CARMELITE
BARRE, VERMONT

W9-ABP-274

THE UNKNOWN GOD?

THEOLOGICAL MEDITATIONS, edited by Hans Küng

Previously Published:

Freedom Today by Hans Küng

THEOLOGICAL MEDITATIONS ·

The Unknown God?

edited with a Preface by HANS KÜNG

1 ARE WE SEARCHING FOR GOD?
by Joseph Möller

2 THE GOD OF THE BEGINNINGS
AND OF TODAY by Herbert Haag

3 ENCOUNTER WITH GOD
by Gotthold Hasenhüttl

SHEED AND WARD · NEW YORK

© Sheed and Ward, Inc., 1966
Part I was originally published in German
under the title Fragen wir nach Gott?,
© Benziger Verlag, Einsiedeln, 1966.
Translated by W. W. White

Part II was originally published in German
under the title Am Morgen der Zeit,
© Benziger Verlag, Einsiedeln, 1964.
It first appeared in English as
The Dawn of Time, © Sheed and Ward, Ltd., 1965.
Translated by M. H. Heelan

Part III was originally published in German
under the title Der unbekannte Gott,
© Benziger Verlag, Einsiedeln, 1965.
Translated by William Whitman

231
Ka

Library of Congress Catalog Card Number 66–22028

Nihil obstat:
    Leo J. Steady, Ph.D., S.T.D.
    Censor Librorum
Imprimatur:
    †Robert F. Joyce
    Bishop of Burlington
    October 1, 1966
The Nihil Obstat and Imprimatur are official decla-
rations that a book or pamphlet is considered to be
free of doctrinal or moral error. No implication is
contained therein that those who have granted the
Nihil Obstat and Imprimatur agree with the contents,
opinions or statements expressed.

Manufactured in the United States of America

ACKNOWLEDGMENTS

The Bible text in this publication is from the Revised Standard Version of the Bible, copyrighted 1946 and 1952 by the Division of Christian Education of the National Council of Churches, and used by permission.

The English translation of passages from Jean-Paul Sartre's play *Les Mouches* is taken from *No Exit and The Flies* by permission of Alfred A. Knopf, Inc. Copyright 1946 by Stuart Gilbert. Also acknowledged is the English translation of passages from *Nausea* by Jean-Paul Sartre. All rights reserved. Reprinted by permission of New Directions Publishing Corporation.

Preface

Is God dead? Anyone who has a little familiarity with the history of theology and spirituality knows that this question is as old as the ages. It seems that every epoch, every generation must answer this question anew for itself. Just as it has been the question of centuries past, so it will remain the question of centuries to come. It will always be the same humanity whose heart threatens to wear out, burdened by lack of faith, doubt, and disillusion. The timelessness of the question, however, makes it not a bit less stimulating, because it is matched by a crucial lack of continuity. This is because the perspective of the question changes from generation to generation, and the answer must be continually rediscovered. In a secular world, where God seems dead, the answer goes forth with greater energy than ever before: God lives. God, the constantly re-hidden and unknown God, is alive!

This fact does not mean that this living God is always experienced in exactly the same way. Certainly He is alive in our milieu, in our lives, in the spirit of our times. But the image of God is subject to change, in fact has changed. And it is not forbidden to us to look for God more in the depths, within our own existence, rather than way up above the highest heavens, to seek Him more inside us than over us.

The *image* of God, the *understanding* of God may change. The *belief* in God should not—I mean that unshakable, trusting belief (shrouded by darkness and withdrawal) in God, our loving Lord. We can conceive of God in divers ways, and in our day there are many suggestions on how to do this. But it all comes down to the basic point that God is living. We can pray only to a living God, not to an abstract principle. We have to ascend to the source from which alone the ultimate answer comes. Thus God will no longer be an unknown God for men of faith, but a known God. It all comes down to this: we must test our image of God not where we give our assent, but where God Himself allows us to find Him—within the testimony of the Bible. Here He shows us where we men of our own day may discover Him for our own lives and for our world as the God who lives, is known and is experienced in His Son, Jesus Christ.

Certainly we cannot oversimplify in this matter. How many people never find the path to this font at all! How many do not find Him because they stand in their own way! Thus, our *first* meditation deals with man today, with his manner of questioning, with his method of experiencing the darkness and the boundaries encompassing his existence. It will be seen that, basically, these elements point to the God who wishes Himself to be experienced in precisely these very modalities. That means, however, that the living God ultimately is viable only by acknowledgment of Him. For this reason, the *second* meditation begins with the words "In the beginning." It begins with the acknowledgment of the Israelites who praised God because they were permitted to live as His creatures, because God, from the very beginning, has been the Lord of mankind. The first three chapters of Genesis begin to pursue the question that is to occupy the entire Bible, namely, what is the relationship between God and man? What is the relationship between God and His world?

The *third* meditation, finally, points out that God puts demands upon man that can be made only by a Living Being. We all should, indeed, be alive, as He is, open for the encounter with our neighbor and, precisely for this reason, witness for the Living Lord who has mercy for us, who receives us exactly the way we come to Him.

If God were unknown, we would also be unknown. Because God is known, we are known to ourselves. If God were dead, we would be, too. Because God lives, so do we. That is the point of this book.

HANS KÜNG

Contents

Preface   8
by Hans Küng

1 Are We Searching for God?   15
   by Joseph Möller

2 The God of the Beginnings and of Today   45
   by Herbert Haag

3 Encounter With God   91
   by Gotthold Hasenhüttl

THE UNKNOWN GOD?

I ARE WE SEARCHING FOR GOD?

by Joseph Möller

TRANSLATED BY W. W. WHITE

1 A Question without an Answer?

In human life there are questions to which we can expect an answer. And there are questions to which we can expect an unequivocal answer. Then, too, there are questions to which no answer is at hand, though perhaps only for the time being. For answers sometimes arise later on, if one has the chance to look back. Some historical problems are clarified by a look backward, though not all. There are questions for which no clear answer is at hand. We don't have an answer to everything. Some people are quick to come up with an answer when really they haven't one. They are uneasy, not having an answer. Thinking back to our school days, we remember examination questions which we couldn't answer. This sort of situation is always difficult.

On the other hand, there are people who don't expect an answer to their questions. There are even some who don't ask until they can hardly expect to have an answer. We can point to people whose entire lives represent a single question, a question without an answer. But next to them stand all of those who have altogether given up raising questions, neither asking nor attempting to find answers. They simply act, making conscious decisions or merely reacting to situations in a primitive manner. In any case, with little thought or speculation. All they do is live and act. Action becomes their answer, the answer to many unresolved questions which one is better off not raising at all. Is there a validity to this sort of attitude? Doesn't action itself represent a form of decision? Why should we raise questions which cannot be met by a comprehensive answer? Or is it a part and parcel of life that we never really receive a comprehensive answer?

Are people today still asking about God? Are they still thinking about God? These questions cannot be answered definitively. For they speak to man's inner self. And the inner self, that which is *really* taking place within a person, escapes us. Not completely, but in its essentials. For one's essential self, his true being, is determined by his stance before God. This area escapes us. In fact, we know little about it within ourselves. A great deal of what we think we know about ourselves is inaccurate, hardly mirroring the truth. This is only too true, whether we want it to be or not. For we maintain that we are basically better than the picture others have of us. It is like us to favor the image we have of ourselves over the image others have of us. Yet we would certainly deny doing this.

Looking at an individual person, we can't tell what his stance is, ultimately, before God. Nor can we say how he, in his inner self, makes his own earnest search for God. It is well at this juncture to establish this fact, for it is a very important one. In this sense, everyone is a secret. This should be stressed, despite anything one might venture to say about

man. For it is not a matter of being able to explain man in
his striving and questioning, and then finally admitting that
he's also something of a secret. In his heart he is a secret, his
heart which is fulfilled in God.

Thus, the only thing we can do is to think over the question we have raised. It is not an abstract, theoretical one. Nor
is it one which we might approach through a new method,
possibly a method yet to be discovered. Nor is the question
an abstract, philosophical one.

It is addressed to modern man in his thought and action.
And thus man himself in his search is placed in the spotlight,
in the middle of the question. Is God still an active force in
this person? An active force in the way that God exists everywhere, if He really *does* exist? Or, rather, is He active in that
man is still seeking Him in thought and thus breaks through
this involvement with self as the center or middle of the question, going on to Him who is considered more than a middle,
more than a beginning or an end.

Are we really still thinking about God? This is a question
to consider. To consider thoughtfully. To meditate upon.
We shouldn't compare statistics. Statistics and methods of
this kind are advisable in a certain sense. They are sometimes
even necessary. Necessary, so that we might not lose sight of
the outer self. For the outer self isn't always an external or
superficial facet of a person. The so-called outer self stems
from the inner. A great deal could be said here about the
outer self, much that warrants serious thought, but also much
that is gratifying; both, one might add, are equally worthy of
thought. This should be stressed, because nowadays many
people hold a pessimistic philosophy of life, whether or not
they admit to doing so. Some because, in their final analysis,

they cannot find a meaning in anything. Others because they have slipped out of a naïvely optimistic attitude (which they may even consider Christian) and don't know where to turn. These people often feel a kinship with those who no longer find meaning in anything, a stronger kinship than they feel toward what is known as Christianity. Finally, there are a considerable number of people who simply go on believing; they really do believe in God, seeking Him, yes, but not actively. They are often laughed at, not only by those who have lost or profess to have lost their faith, but by those who do more searching than actual believing, in contrast to those of simple faith whose belief is strong but whose search is feeble—perhaps for want of ideals. They could be called naïve. But often, without their really being conscious of it, their naïvety contains great wisdom. The wisdom which will be more of an answer to those seeking feebly than to those seeking too intensively.

2 Godlessness and the Search for God

Are people today still thinking about God? This is a thought-provoking question. One could point to the staggering growth of atheism as a world outlook. This growth is incontestable if one looks at man as a whole, at his outer self. But we really don't know how many people are atheists at heart. I wouldn't venture to say. My only question would be whether the atheism abroad today hasn't been with us for hundreds or even thousands of years, possibly in a latent form. The history of western civilization, whether truly Christian or Christian in name alone, offers us the records of thinkers who have been or could be cited as atheists. Such thinkers and such currents have been on the rise in modern times. This isn't to say that our epoch necessarily turns man away from God. I wouldn't go so far as to say that. I'm merely maintaining that there are and have been thinkers and currents of this kind: someone wants to devote himself to man, and he turns away from God. Christianity is found to be insufficiently human (although God's Son became a *human*), and so another turns away from God. Or the breakdown occurs when many Christians fail to live up to their ideals; then still another feels he must turn against the religion as a whole. Simply be man, without Christ, without God. Ideas which were once the principles of individual thinkers are now the actions of millions of people. Many of these people claim to be Christians just as before. Are they still searching for God?

Finally, it should be remembered that a second historical process has developed adjacent to that of the purportedly or truly Christian West, and that it goes back thousands of years, paralleling that of the Christian West for the last two thousand years. By nature, Christianity couldn't play the same role in the history of these peoples as it did in our own. Thus, these peoples whom we—often disguising our arrogance and casualness in a cloak of "Christian" love— have termed heathen are also susceptible to the phenomenon of atheism, and in a way which merits our careful consideration. This term says nothing about the manner or extent of their search for God. Today we live side-by-side with these peoples. They belong to our time and our world, for the "heathens" no longer live at a distance, on the periphery, objects of our envy or pity. Together with us they form the world. We don't know to whom the future belongs. For

these peoples, discounting exceptions, Christianity is of no
real importance. We can't tell how they stand before God.
But they are aware of their growing political power. He who
is to become the more powerful of the two isn't preoccupied
with becoming the more humble of the two before God. Yet,
we do not pursue humility either, we who are getting po-
litically weaker all the time.

This warrants further critical attention. The phenomena
are known and are brought up again and again. As technology
increases and as what we call *World* grows more powerful,
man is more and more inclined to merge into this World
and lose himself therein. To many people today, the power
of God seems to be little more than a peculiar form of powerlessness, while the world goes on pursuing its hard, inexorable
course. Political life is one of the areas where this holds true.
Of course, this deafness of politics to God is a phenomenon
permeating the whole of human history, and it bears thinking about, although we should not allow it to lead us into
resignation. What we might consider here is why God seems
hardly to exist in current political life. This may have been
different with many periods and peoples; a critical and objective look backward into history will dissuade us from seeing simple opposites in the "Christian West" and today's
increasingly prevalent atheism. It is probably true that the influence of Christ is less and less perceptible on the social
scene and that God's name is hardly ever pronounced anymore. An inner-worldly thought has come to the fore. Is this
a thought which still looks toward God? Here again we have
the difficult question which speaks of man's heart. It seems
to be much more important to try to explain everything, once
and for all, without God: technology, progress, social legisla-

tion, society, State and history. There is nothing wrong with this sort of explanation (this should be clearly understood) as long as it remains technical and scientific.

But it becomes questionable when it comes forward with the implied or explicit claim to be an explanation sufficient unto itself. The strange thing here is that, although the life expectancy of man has been increased by decades, hidden anxieties have also increased. Not just anxiousness about death but, perhaps even more, an anxiousness about life. Strange? Or simply logical? The clearest expression of man's technical power along with his powerlessness is his fear of the atomic bomb. Coupled with anxiety, serenity is apt to wane. And sometimes it may seem that, in contrast to the modern atheist who would like to feel that the question of God is filed away (and possibly in contrast to the Christian who has resigned, as well), the so-called heathen whom we hear so little about in the history of western civilization is the more dedicated to the search for God.

3 The Inner and Outer Life

Here is something to consider: today there are many people who call themselves Christians, but who are Christian in name only. And perhaps not merely for reasons having to do with the outer self. Perhaps simply because they find themselves living within a certain historical tradition and are loath to separate themselves from it. They needn't be thought of as out-and-out unbelievers. It's just that the search for God doesn't seem to be the central question of their lives. On the whole, discussion in social intercourse today rarely centers on

God or on those who are seeking Him. One could almost say that, for many people today, the only things discussed are those which aren't worth talking about.

But is this true of our period alone? Was it basically different at other times? What was the situation when Christianity stepped forward as the outer, dominating power, seeking to play the leading role in the social structure? In the Middle Ages, was God really the central question in people's lives? Was Reformation man concerned uniquely with the question of God?

This question prompts us to attack the problem from a sharply new angle. There is a great deal of material at hand— even material from the outer life, from World—which can be brought to bear against an excessively pessimistic outlook. First of all, one can point out that, despite everything, the search for God has had a larger place in the history of modern thought than one usually allows. The search, at least, has been pursued seriously by many thinkers—in fact, I should say by most thinkers, right up to the present time. Among modern thinkers the number of confirmed atheists is disproportionately small. It is very difficult to tell the degree to which the people living under a dictatorship and whose State religion is atheism have really become confirmed atheists themselves. There are no statistics at all to help us here. For many of these people there is only one possibility left, one freedom—that of concealing their true relationship to this question. This may occur frequently among our own peoples, too: a person rarely speaking about God, but continuing nevertheless to seek Him in his heart. One can have strong feelings here and bring considerable material to bear, yet darkness shrouds the Ultimate. And this remains so, despite the close studies into the matter, studies so numerous that no one can read them all. Despite all the religious and spiritual histories. Neither Spengler, nor Toynbee, nor Jaspers, nor depth psychology are of real help to us. For our question points into the *Deep*, which reveals itself to us only through suggestions and intimations.

The history of mankind's search for God can never be recorded literally. Man possesses the enormous power we call freedom. Historical laws exist only in a qualified sense. There is every possibility that man in his steady technical and cultural growth will continue to increase his knowledge and capabilities. This may startle us if we look back over the progress in science and culture during the last hundred years. Man runs the risk of losing contact with his inner self in the course of this growth. In pointing this out, we don't mean to ascribe a negative value to this development as such. Technical progress doesn't necessarily spell the destruction of inner life; in fact, it proceeds from man's inner life, and only through man's inner life is it possible. It is also possible that, in the course of a growth process of this kind, man will have a greater and greater tendency to return to himself, in that the passage of years brings him into closer touch with its borders. As thinkers and as believers, we shouldn't let ourselves fall prey to a religious faith in progress (nor to an exalted faith of this kind: "We're going to be able to do away with hunger and misery; prosperity will come to all; people will settle their differences," and so forth). But we should be no less prone to ascribe a negative value to progress in our outer life. The rise of technology doesn't necessarily turn man into a machine, into a robot or a creature suited only to the dictatorship of a collective society, whatever its form may be. This grouping of individuals into masses which is going on nearly everywhere in the world can have important consequences for man. But it can also lead to his inner refusal to submit to it, even when he has or seems to have succumbed to it. Is this only a theoretical possibility, a daydream? Hardly. History knows no necessary laws.

Will man become more and more collectivized? Will the question of his essential nature dwindle and die? Will the search for God suffer the same fate? We can only consider this question and throw light on several phenomena which might serve as a partial answer. And again, these phenomena point to man. Basically man is and remains a questioning and questionable creature. Basically he is one who asks "Why?" And in doing so, he is a thinking creature. He sees himself as one involved in a beginning, a beginning which is ever renewed. And he sees an end approaching, for one day he will die. But this man, living in space and time, and versed in it, limited, too, by a beginning and an end, is a creature whose questions extend into the realm before the beginning and beyond the end. Man doesn't simply accept that which lies between the beginning and the end at its face value, that which we call life. He searches it for its meaning. He doesn't merely put up with the world around him; he forms it. He builds his understanding of it. He surpasses it in thought. Man is the only creature to inquire after meaning or to act with free will, even if his field of action is constantly reduced. Man is a creature that cannot be explained by virtue of his simple presence on earth, by his simply existing. At the same time, he is possessed of a curiosity to learn all he can about the world around him, ever seeking a view of the whole. Man cannot explain this desire simply through the fact of his existence. Man is only himself when he is more than a mere creature of his environment. He is a creature whose very being is oriented toward something Ultimate. Man is attuned to something which exceeds the details, encounters and events of this world, which exceeds any possible event in this world.

But is this really true? Does man wonder about the things going on around him? Aren't there many people who live for today, possibly for tomorrow and even the day after tomorrow, but whose interest and curiosity end there? Is man really the creature whose questions extend into the realm before the beginning and beyond the end? Aren't there many people who can't be bothered, who are content to take life as it comes, making peace with it as best they can? Life, they say, is difficult enough as it is. Why make it harder by asking difficult questions? Is man really a creature who would like to have his existence explained? Is there an answer which would explain our existence in such a way that it would somehow be equivalent to the fact that we're here? We are here. That is a fact, and no one contests it. And our disappearance from the earth a long time hence is another fact awaiting us. No one contests that either, for it is incontestable. Yet, one doesn't want to believe it in relation to oneself. Being and the cessation of being—if we look at this question as it applies directly to ourselves and not as a problem applied to others, we wonder whether it can be met with an answer which isn't itself subject to further question. Is man really one to inquire into the area beyond his death? Couldn't it be a token of great wisdom simply to take one's death as a fact and to exert as much control over one's life as one can? One day we shall probably have to resign ourselves, if a sweet and early death doesn't spare us the trouble.

These thoughts are not simply abstract speculation. We know that there are people who shrink from final questions of this kind. Partly because this sort of inquiry is burdensome, partly because it is uncomfortable, partly because it doesn't seem to terminate in clear and final understanding. One avoids these questions. To modern man, this avoidance seems suitable and right. Here one could almost say that, in an odd way, modern man is in a position to practice this avoidance. Why? Many attempts have already been made to explain why. One cause has already been mentioned. What we call *World* has become more and more powerful through the development of modern thought and the progress of technology. And man's consciousness of his freedom and of his ability to affect many areas which were heretofore beyond his control have made him more powerful, too. We have alluded to the idea that, since Kant, inquiry beyond the world as it is presented to us is considered a doubtful business and is consigned to faith alone. Not to a faith which might be little more than unquestioning belief, but to one which is genuine, grounded in theology. But the difficulty here is that such a faith somehow seems to do nothing more than differentiate itself from reason, since reason is no longer qualified to pursue inquiry beyond the present, beyond the beginning and the end. Thus reason and faith are cast as antithetical elements and run the risk of forming a sharp contradiction. To an outsider, faith must seem to be little more than a state of despair which is supposed to conquer despair. No allowance is made for its ability to justify this claim. We should not fail to recognize that, from the beginning of the nineteenth century right up to the present time, a school of thought has been steadily gaining adherents, a school which maintains that reason and knowledge should restrict themselves to the given, to the empirical. And, for the "thinking" man, that's as far as it goes. There's nothing beyond—nothing, that is, if we refer to our faculty of reason. (Should a person believe that the omnipotence of God lies hidden within this *Nothing*, or *Nothingness*, may he do so in peace. But he shouldn't importune his neighbors with this faith. For the experiences which led him to embrace it are incommunicable. Nor are his intellective reasons sufficient; yet, modern man often thinks in this vein.)

But if Nothingness is the determining power we must contend with, then our questions nevertheless do press beyond the world and lead into ourselves at the same time. For it can happen that the power of this Nothingness seems to be the leading element shaping our lives. Thus, one would have to decide between what we might call a negative nihilism—which tends toward pessimism, despair, or resignation—and a so-called positive nihilism as advocated by Nietzsche. This latter outlook sees new value in man by virtue of the Nothingness surrounding him and has a new positive image of his potential. It refers man to his potential as a superman.

Now, we have a certain scepticism toward this notion of a superman. Not just from the Reich which was to last a thousand years but which lasted only twelve. But simply from the fact that there is no such thing. And it's quite doubtful that a superman will ever come about, whatever our leading biologists may predict. But, finally, one could maintain that nineteenth- and twentieth-century philosophy has produced currents which see man in another light. Here one could cite the different directions taken within theologic thought as well as a philosophic thought derived, in part, from theology. No less important, one could cite the thought of German idealism which broke through the confines of the world and of the concrete *I* to distinguish the finite from the infinite. One could speak of phenomenology and the way it was carried forward by Husserl to terminate in Heidegger's philosophy of *being*, a philosophy in which transcendence of being is acquired through breaking through and out of this world, even if being, in this context, is not considered divine. One could point out that, everything considered, transcendence belongs to reason even in Jaspers' thought, and that man is therefore pursuing this inquiry into and beyond everything within himself, even if the real meaning of this transcendence is philosophically not altogether accessible to us as Jaspers sees it. Here, again, we find ourselves thinking in terms of a history of philosophy. It is important to avoid being one-sided in presenting these ideas, to reach them through the initial thesis and counter-thesis. Here, too, neither the argument nor counter-argument has clear-cut conclusions if we limit ourselves to the context of a history of philosophy. What *is* clear is the knottiness of the question.

Having focused our inquiry on man in his thinking and questioning self, we proceed with our problem by examining three phenomena which merit consideration: the phenomenon of World, the phenomenon of human Freedom, and, finally, the phenomenon known as Nothingness.

4 World and God

For twentieth-century man, the world is important in a special sense. I'm not referring to his knowledge of the staggering distances within the cosmos. Nor am I thinking of space travel which, considering the dimensions of the universe, is limited to the vicinity of the earth. It's not my intent to speak of how many billions of years the cosmos has existed nor of the age of our earth. Nor am I broaching the question of whether science has indications that this cosmos may one day perish. These are all purely scientific questions. When we say that, for twentieth-century man, the world is important in a special manner, we are referring to what he must contend with, what he must master, what he must deal with on a day-to-day basis. We don't mean simply the sum total of what man has to contend with; we also mean man, himself. We mean man to the extent that he forms the world, and we mean his surroundings as a whole to the extent that he makes them up. Through learning how to improve and master his surroundings to such an amazing degree, man is continually finding himself before new plans, facing new tasks. And all this pressures him in a quite specific way, the pressure penetrating into him, determining his very life. In his thought, desire and planning he seems himself bound to what he calls World. World, then, isn't simply what man must contend with. It is what permeates him. In this way, World is a phenomenon which characterizes and determines human life. It has always existed. But it has grown in power as man has expanded his capabilities. It is neutral in itself. It is bad only when it—that is, when man—basically rejects God (hence the negative value of the World in the Gospel according to St. John).

Man, in feeling himself constantly pressured and threatened by the World, in knowing that this pressure and threat lie within him (for things, as such, don't threaten us), is in danger of seeing himself merely as a phenomenon in pressuring, threatening surroundings. He no longer turns his inquiry inward. He becomes increasingly estranged from his own being and, with it, from the being of his person. The self-estrangement of man becomes a meaningful term here. The self-estrangement of man, even though all this planning and accomplishment and technology depend on him. Technology doesn't merely depend on him; it has permeated him to such an extent that no one can tell who has the upper hand. I'm not thinking only of the possibility of the malfunction of an electronic brain touching off a war. The question is only too real when man and human life are considered from a purely technical viewpoint. When man is regarded merely as a creature who has to work and who must be looked after, once his work is done. Thus the real self-estrangement does not arise from man's estrangement from the product of his work (though, this, too, is a case of estrangement), but from his regarding the product of his work as his being, seeing himself in this light alone. This situation occurs whenever technology gains the upper hand. And whenever administrating becomes the *sole* activity, human sentiment disappears. There must be a great deal of administrating going on beyond the Iron Curtain, where men are crowded in upon each other, where distances shrink and the over-all structure of life is complicated to the limit. The disappearance of what is truly human, man's estrangement from himself, represents a phenomenon of our times and should be weighed with utmost seriousness. Thus, the question of whether a world structure of this kind might somehow suffice unto itself is not just a question to be debated in the abstract. It is also a question of a general human attitude toward life.

5 Freedom and God

Can't we try to resolve this question of man's attitude toward life by appealing to man's freedom? Isn't it true that man in his freedom—and only man in freedom—can stand up to this march of technology? Today we stress this freedom again and again. Contrary to the philosophy of dictatorship which takes freedom away from the individual, we stress man's right to freedom. Is it enough to stress freedom of this kind? For what does freedom really consist of? Is it just a standing up against despotism and class rule, against the State's encroachment on the individual, against the power of the collective society swallowing up the identity of the individual? Does it stand up for a right? Which right? Certainly the individual doesn't have unlimited freedom. It's not simply a question of the limitations which his gifts, milieu and capabilities impose on his decisions. The individual doesn't have unlimited freedom because he lives in a community with his fellow man. Because he must respect the rights of his neighbor. Therefore, should our conception of freedom be merely a negation of the power of an absolutist State, but more or less meaningless beyond that, despite all that is said about the freedom to foster a personal identity?

Of course, there are certain rights I couldn't deny the individual man. I must recognize them as his. And so must the State. Only when they are respected do we have true justice. Extreme injustice reigns behind the Iron Curtain where these rights are not upheld in the name of justice, but are destroyed. However, what does this freedom really consist of? Simply the phenomenon of my being able to make a basic choice in favor of one thing over another? Or merely the phenome-

non that, in spite of recognizing all my bounds and commit-
ments, I can go on making new decisions and must go on
making them? Or does freedom go only so far as to mean
that modern man, though living, more or less, in a collective
society, has certain individual rights he can call his own?

Man does possess true freedom. He possesses it because he
is more than simply a piece of the World. Because he can
speak, because he can say the word *Thou*, because all of his
plans and actions are a dialogue with something beyond himself. Man is not just a unification of molecules, atoms and
elementary particles. And he is more than a creature as yet
without identity. Man possesses a power within him which,
at the same time, lifts him up and out of himself. He is free
because spirit is the determining force within him. There is
indecision in the mineral kingdom, and in the animal kingdom there is the power of life and of the senses. But man
alone can have volition, even when he is being held prisoner.
Man alone can say No, even when he is condemned to
death. Man alone can associate the Manifest and the Un-
manifest in thought. Man alone creates civilization and takes
part in forming the world. Poetry, thought and artistic creation are proper to him alone. All quantitative and purely
biological ways of looking at man fall short of the mark here.
Man is free.

Both power and freedom are subject to misuse. This isn't
limited to the individual who will consult his freedom and
go ahead and do as he pleases. This doesn't mean simply he
who consults his freedom so he can plow ahead with what
suits his plans best. The misuse lies, first and foremost, in
the individual's considering his freedom *the* freedom. The
misuse can lie in man's freedom simply seeming to be *the*

freedom. Man is free. But he isn't free in that certain rights have been given him. He is free because freedom is the determining force in his being as a man. It is given man along with his being, and precisely to that end. And there is always a tie hidden within human freedom. This tie isn't exactly a limiting of an absolute *I* (there is no such thing), but is the original relationship pointing to a second person, a *Thou*, and to the community. Without such a tie, freedom doesn't exist. This doesn't mean that one should emphasize this tie, casting it as an out-and-out obligation so that one can have a device for doing away with freedom. It means only that, in the human context, freedom and commitment have mutual reference in one another. It is a tragedy in the history of freedom to consider freedom as the absolute freedom of man. Man's attempt to free himself from all ties in the quest for absolute freedom is nothing more than his attempt to jump over his own shadow so he can be free of himself. And this would amount to the disappearance of what we know as human.

A free man, striving for absolute freedom, estranges himself from himself to the same degree as the man who sees himself as a mere cog in a collective society. The only man capable of attaining freedom is he who is aware of his inner nature. Man's inner nature is governed and dominated by boundaries. Freedom of the human spirit is always associated with a Thou. And in this association alone does man discover himself. The world over, man lives among his fellows, bound to them, restricted by them as well. Communal living of this kind is more than the communal existence of just any creature taken at random. It is the togetherness of one man with another in the Thou relationship. This true, pure interrelatedness with one's fellow man is characteristic of human freedom—interrelatedness with a Thou. The attitude which not only knows itself in the hands of a Thou, but respects and affirms the Thou.

What does all this have to do with our question? A great deal, it seems to me. For only through freedom does man become truly man. Through freedom he must break through the World structure. He must break through the World from within in order to form the World. But man becomes man only if he returns to himself at the same time. That which is formed in the world in which we live is formed by man. But we have to ask whether man's inner life is just as critical to him as his forming of the World. Man can grow superficial and regard himself and his fellows as objects. But he can do this only because he possesses a Within. But this means that any misuse of human freedom has consequences for that freedom. It is limited, clearly so. This is clearer than the fact that freedom exists in the first place. (For we are always having our doubts about this freedom because it is so limited; we seldom run across it in a way that convinces us of its nature, once and for all.)

How can man be at peace with himself while possessing this limited freedom? How can he be at peace with himself while spanning these two opposites, freedom and commitment? He is faced with a clear picture of himself through spanning these opposites; he experiences his freedom through the constant limitations imposed upon it. But he also experiences himself as the synthesizer of these opposites. Man must direct his search inward, asking what the impelling force is which sets these two opposites within him. How easy it is to say that this man must direct his search inward. But many don't raise this question at all. They just live life as it comes. But the question takes on meaning when man isn't at peace with himself, when he realizes that he can't find peace in himself. And man won't find peace with himself, for he isn't at peace with himself, because he is and remains incomplete even in what he can accomplish, even in his freedom. Again and again he tries to side-step the troubling question of where he came from and where he is going. But he can't do this forever. He asks why he came to be, why he is living, why he must always go on searching. He asks what is impelling his life forward, in his harboring these opposites within himself. It can't be man himself, for he doesn't enjoy power over his own life; he remains limited. It can't be World, for human freedom surpasses World. One can't reduce man's freedom to World, still less to matter. Therefore, the impelling force, that which gives his life its shape, lies neither with man, nor World, nor matter. Might it not lie with Nothingness? Or with an absolute freedom, a freedom which is no longer human, where man's tie with a Thou would finally be done away with and where fulfillment would be reached through making a commitment to this freedom, itself of a superhuman nature?

6 Nothingness and God

Or might not this impelling force, which gives life its shape, lie with Nothingness, after all? Could it be that, in the last analysis, our freedom and thus our being as men are governed by Nothingness? But what is that supposed to mean, by Nothingness? That we don't know the meaning of

our existence? That the meaning of our existence seems somehow dark? Simply the meaning of our existence or our very
existence itself? For do we know who we really and truly are?
And if we did know, would we want to presume ourselves
capable of bearing such knowledge? Isn't this what a so-called
positive nihilism claims to do, that is, propose that we bear
up under our existence without our knowing who we really
are and what our existence means? It is worth while here to
give serious thought to this claim, regardless of the particular
persuasion one brings to bear in trying to learn the meaning
of life.

True nihilism aspires to more than that. It casts real doubts
on this meaning. It expects man to raise the question of the
meaning of life; and it expects him to expect to do without
an answer to the question. But not simply to do without an
answer through mean resignation, but to answer with Nothingness or the Nothingness. Yet Nothingness doesn't exist,
or at least it doesn't seem to; for then it would be meaningless to speak of a Nothingness. But we exist. Thus all forms
of nihilism face this contradiction: of referring to a Nothingness, on the one hand, and of having to recognize man's
being, on the other. Therefore, all forms of nihilism, if they
don't choose flight in suicide, necessarily lead back to man—
specifically to man's being which exists and yet shouldn't
exist at all. And since man does exist, all forms of nihilism
set this limited man as some sort of absolute. In the face of
Nothingness, which doesn't exist, man must be absolute.
For nothing is supposed to exist beyond man living in this
world. Even a form of nihilism hoping to design a superman
refers back to man once again. For it is man who is to design
or construct this superman. Thus it is logical that, with

Sartre, whose concern is not with a superman, man's freedom is established as an absolute, man himself is freedom, and his existence is formed as freedom. If God doesn't exist, all we have left is man. All we have left is the paradox of setting this limited man up as an absolute. And with it the paradox of no longer holding the Absolute as absolute. But there's another possibility, that of not simply setting one man or another up as an absolute, but of looking for a new Absolute. Could it be found in a collective society, either in a present-day model or a classless society of the future?

Belief in absolute freedom is at all times a threat to belief in a collective society. This is quite logical. We know that the question of a collective society of this kind is a ticklish matter, as is the question of freedom, if freedom claims to be absolute human freedom and doesn't bear in mind the tie which is inevitably implied. Freedom is true freedom only if it is conscious of its obligations, its obligations to a Thou, its obligations to society, its obligations to mankind. And are these obligations an answer if they are not finally an answer in God? Without these obligations before God, doesn't freedom prompt one toward arbitrary, abusive action, possibly even toward despotism? And if we're going to have action of this sort, why shouldn't a certain group or class carry it out in uncompromising terms. This talk about absolute human freedom leads to the destruction of freedom. It leads to the disappearance of obligations and the triumph of arbitrariness. And why shouldn't arbitrariness triumph, if freedom recognizes no obligations?

We don't want to oversimplify. The man who takes his freedom seriously, who strives to make the right decision, somehow reaches forward into a Nothingness in the course

of exercising his freedom. Yet, even in striving to act responsibly, we can't be sure we'll totally subdue this Nothingness.
From the outset we have no guarantee that Good always
prevails. Evil, which appeals to man's freedom and autonomy,
wields enormous power. It is neither easy nor pleasant to act
responsibly at all times. Moreover, quite often it doesn't lead
to success. The combination of a cool-headed egoistic aim, a
clever calculation of what will turn out successfully, plus
high-mindedness (whether genuine or feigned) is much more
attractive, much more apt to bring results. One can even associate this behavior with "Christianity"; and no wonder the
non-Christian sneers at this association. It makes a mockery
of Christianity, although it holds good everywhere: Christians behaving this way with astonishing alacrity, frequently
not even concealing their actions, but backing them up with
sober, calculating arguments. Often it may seem that Christianity doesn't belong to this world, coming on the scene only
when success is lacking. Nietzsche analyzed this question
thoroughly, and only a Christianity whose ideals are em-
bodied in action can stand up to refute him.

As free men, we are summoned to our responsibilities.
But we aren't offered security in the bargain. As free men,
insecurity is our lot. We can never get a really solid grip on
the future. Things don't turn out exactly as we would have
them. Some do, but the Whole is more than we can handle.
History affords us a clear indication of this: however responsibly we may act, things never turn out wholly as we would
have them. This Not aspect of the future, this Not-to-Be-
Dominated aspect of the future is part and parcel of our life.
Not just the Nothingness of death, which all of us shrink
from in one way or another. There is a Nothingness present

in our very lives. In our thought and action we men reach out into an area unlike the one in which we live. As thinking and acting men, we reach out into an area unlike the workaday world. And we are too easily inclined to dismiss it as Nothingness. To limit ourselves to everyday affairs, doing the next thing or what seems to be the most necessary thing, without considering that which seems to be the most necessary thing may really be the least necessary.

And what about Nothingness? Is it supposed to conceal the Real within itself? If we exist and live, if we are free men, should our calling consist in living in reference to a hidden area? It's not quite the idea that we're living on this earth now and at some future time will belong to a Beyond. But rather, it's more that this so-called Beyond is actually what makes the present world possible in the first place, i.e., our self, our being, our life. In the final analysis, this apparent Nothingness which stands facing us with our destiny in its hands must be more than we are ourselves. It must be more comprehensive. If, as thinking men, we have the strength to inquire into ourselves, if we can summon the strength to search this darkness, we shall have to say that this apparent darkness is the true Vast. This spanning of the opposites—freedom and commitment—which characterizes man, and the limitedness of human existence are explicable only if this darkness we search really constitutes the final freedom to which we owe our being and our life.

Now we have reached the frontier of our thought, frontier in that what we are dealing with here doesn't resemble the day-to-day life in which we put our faith. But do we really put our faith so completely in day-to-day life? Do we know what it actually is? Doesn't this question lead us back into the depths of human being, into an area which man can't solidly grasp? Doesn't it open that area which forms man?

Here we are speaking of God. And because we are free men and because man is a person, we are speaking of a personal God. To be sure, even an answer of this kind leaves our question in darkness. We have come to the silence of God. What we are getting at here isn't a single pat answer to all inquiry, to all our desire and volition. The question we are considering leads us straight into darkness. And it must, necessarily, if God is really God. For God as God is always a mystery to us, not any sort of mystery, but the basic mystery of our lives. The basic mystery of our freedom and our world, for God is basically more than our freedom and our world. The idea that God is our fellow man has attracted a certain following, but it is insufficient, for God is more than the fellow man met by our thought, wish and conception. For God is the Never-to-be-Seized, the Never-to-be-Grasped. Therefore, reference to God's silence should never be a substitute for unsolved problems, unanswered questions. This silence of God is also His inscrutable action. An "action" in relation to which even the greatest human achievements pale into insignificance.

The aim of our inquiry is to tune our ear to the area of Nothingness, to become inwardly still, inwardly calm, and to hear the answer which alone can give us God. Through faith we know that God appeared to us in his Son Jesus Christ and that an answer is given to us in that form. We can't obtain this answer through our knowledge, only through listening. So the inquiry into man's inner life and the question of what freedom really is comes down to listening, to a readiness to receive the word of God. We cannot force the word of God through human powers. All we can do is hold ourselves ready, in true inquiry. Only in this do we escape the danger of estranging ourselves from ourselves.

A Christian should know about the meaning of Nothingness. A Christian should know about the transient nature of definitions. And this, through faith in the power of the word of God which is mightier than all words of man. And the Christian knows about Nothingness through thought which passes beyond all frontiers, but which is unable to grasp the Ungraspable. Thus the Christian stands in dialogue with the thinking man who is continually directing his inquiry beyond everything mankind has devised, who is tempted toward resignation, but who doesn't succumb to it. Should the light of God's freedom—God's freedom which exceeds human freedom and thought—shine into what we so often call dark Nothingness, into what so many men see as dark Nothingness? And might we find our own true freedom then, as we realize that ours is derived from and contained within His?

Will man become freer or enslave himself further? This question may seem murky to us, but the freedom has been given us not only to raise the question, but to seek an answer. Are we still trying to do so? Or have we fallen into resignation already? If so, then for a long time, despite our talk every day about freedom, we have been laying the best possible groundwork for slavery and the collective society.

2 THE GOD OF THE BEGINNINGS AND OF TODAY

by Herbert Haag

TRANSLATED BY M. H. HEELAN

1 In the Beginning God Created . . .

In the beginning God created the heavens and the earth. The earth was without form and void, and darkness was upon the face of the deep; and the Spirit of God was moving over the face of the waters.

And God said, "Let there be light"; and there was light. And God saw that the light was good; and God separated the light from the darkness. God called the light Day, and the darkness he called Night. And there was evening and there was morning, one day.

And God said, "Let there be a firmament in the midst of the waters, and let it separate the waters from the waters." And God made the firmament and separated the waters which were under the firmament from the waters which were above the firmament. And it was so. And God called the firmament Heaven. And there was evening and there was morning, a second day.

And God said, "Let the waters under the heavens be

gathered together into one place, and let the dry land appear." And it was so. God called the dry land Earth, and the waters that were gathered together he called Seas. And God saw that it was good. And God said, "Let the earth put forth vegetation, plants yielding seed, and fruit trees bearing fruit in which is their seed, each according to its kind, upon the earth." And it was so. The earth brought forth vegetation, plants yielding seed according to their own kinds, and trees bearing fruit in which is their seed, each according to its kind. And God saw that it was good. And there was evening and there was morning, a third day.

And God said, "Let there be lights in the firmament of the heavens to separate the day from the night; and let them be for signs and for seasons and for days and years, and let them be lights in the firmament of the heavens to give light upon the earth." And it was so. And God made the two great lights, the greater light to rule the day, and the lesser light to rule the night; he made the stars also. And God set them in the firmament of the heavens to give light upon the earth, to rule over the day and over the night, and to separate the light from the darkness. And God saw that it was good. And there was evening and there was morning, a fourth day.

And God said, "Let the waters bring forth swarms of living creatures, and let birds fly above the earth across the firmament of the heavens." So God created the great sea monsters and every living creature that moves, with which the waters swarm, according to their kinds and every winged bird according to its kind. And God saw that it was good. And God blessed them, saying, "Be fruitful and multiply and fill the waters in the seas, and let birds multiply on the earth." And there was evening and there was morning, a fifth day.

And God said, "Let the earth bring forth living creatures according to their kinds: cattle and creeping things and beasts of the earth according to their kinds." And it was so. And God made the beasts of the earth according to their kinds and the cattle according to their kinds, and everything that creeps upon the ground according to its kind. And God saw that it was good.

Then God said, "Let us make man in our image, after our likeness; and let them have dominion over the fish of the sea, and over the birds of the air, and over the cattle, and over all the earth, and over every creeping thing that creeps upon the earth." So God created man in his own image, in the image of God he created him; male and female he created them . . . And God saw everything that he had made, and, behold, it was very good. And there was evening and there was morning, a sixth day.

Thus the heavens and the earth were finished, and all the host of them. And on the seventh day God finished his work which he had done, and he rested on the seventh day from all his work which he had done. So God blessed the seventh day and hallowed it, because on it God rested from all his work which he had done in creation (Gen. i.1–27, 31; ii.1–3).

How often is our peace of mind disturbed by questions which seem—at the time—to demand a conclusive, or at least a comforting answer! But a moment comes for each of us—the moment of truth—when we realize that only one of these many questions is really important in the long run, and that is, "How do I stand in relation to God?" It is a question for God and for myself, and both of us have our answer. God gives me his answer in Holy Scripture, which is his word. My own conscience gives me my answer.

God tells me in Holy Scripture how I stand in relation to him. Holy Scripture is a bulky book, made up of many very different parts, and yet every page of it deals with only two subjects—God and man. But the Bible does not deal with these two subjects by placing God on one side and man on the other, as if it meant to present us with a theology and an anthropology. It does not pretend to be a systematic study of God and a systematic study of man. When we say that the Bible treats of God and man, the significant word is "and." The Bible treats of God and man *in conjunction*; it deals with the relationship of God to man and of the relationship of man to God. The whole of the Bible is concerned with these relationships, but its very first pages deal with them in a special way, and it is in those first pages that we propose to look for the answer to our question, "How do I stand in relation to God?"

The very first sentence of the Bible, indeed, gives us the conclusive answer to our question. "In the beginning," it says, "God created the heavens and the earth." This opening sentence introduces the biblical account of creation, which fills the first pages of Holy Scripture. Our modern age is, of course, disposed to look askance at the biblical account of creation. Our times being what they are, these first pages of Holy Scripture provoke frank comment. Our view of the world is far removed from that of the age and land in which they were written. Science has since provided us with a very different idea of the cosmos and of man's place in it. The feelings of a person who is about to undertake a journey into space are certainly not the same as those of an unsophisticated observer, like our biblical writer, who looks up at the sun and moon in childlike wonder and tells us that God created the greater light and the lesser light and the stars also. Does the Bible still convey anything to us when it says that God made the world in six days, that on the first day he made the light, on the second the air, on the third the sea and the land-mass and its vegetation, on the fourth the heavenly bodies, on the fifth the fishes and birds, and on the sixth the land animals—and man?

We might reply to this question offhand by pointing out that the biblical account is not entirely naïve from the standpoint of modern science. For modern science and the inspired author of the first chapter of Genesis agree that man was the last to appear on the scene. While our earth is perhaps 4,500 million years old, man has been on it for a mere million years at most. Long before he arrived, certain species of animals had appeared on the earth, lived on it for millions of years, and then disappeared. We have only to think of the saurians, monster reptiles over 60 ft. long and up to 40 tons in weight, which appeared on the earth some 200 million years before our time and disappeared about 60 million years ago. We could accept all this as being true and still maintain that nothing in it runs counter to the biblical account of creation. For it would have been clear to us from the very outset that the Bible has its own way of putting things, and that this way is entirely different from that of modern science. The Bible is not primarily concerned with the *manner* in which the world came into being or the *matter* of which it is com-

posed. A superficial reading of the account of creation might
incline us to think otherwise, but in fact the question behind
it all and the only question with which the Bible is concerned
is, "What is the relationship between God and man?"

The Bible's answer to this question is to be found—as we
have said—in its very first words: "In the beginning God
created the heavens and the earth." By "the heavens and the
earth" Holy Scripture means what we usually express by the
word "universe" (from the Latin *universum*), which denotes
the sum total of everything that exists, outside of God; or,
as we say in the Nicene Creed: "*Credo in unum Deum,
Patrem omnipotentem, factorem coeli et terrae, visibilium
omnium et invisibilium*"—"I believe in one God, the al-
mighty Father, maker of heaven and earth, of all things
visible and invisible." All these visible and invisible things,
Holy Writ tells us, were *created* by God; all of them came
from his hand, each a being from his being, a light from his
light, a life from his life. They did not escape from his hand
or fall out of it, by accident; he deliberately created them.
The account of creation keeps on repeating that God spoke
and commanded that something should come into existence,
and his command was obeyed. God creates by his *word*, and
the word is the expression of the *will*. The Bible depicts the
word that God spoke as a messenger sent out by him on a
mission, a messenger who never fails to fulfil that mission:

> For as the rain and the snow come down from heaven,
> and return not thither but water the earth,
> making it bring forth and sprout,
> giving seed to the sower and bread to the eater,
> so shall my word be that goes forth from my mouth;
> it shall not return to me empty,

but it shall accomplish that which I purpose,
and prosper in the thing for which I sent it.

—(Isa. lv.10f)

These words of the prophet are almost contemporary with
the account of creation. That explains why the latter is at
such pains to stress that creation is the result of God's active
will; the sun exists because he willed it should exist, the earth
likewise; and I am here also because he willed I should exist,
a life from his life and a light from his light.

God, we are told, created all these visible and invisible
things in the beginning. We might well despair of getting
any further with so vague a word as "beginning," and we
should so dearly like to know how many millions or thousands
of millions of years ago God began his work of creation! We
know now that rays of lights from the galaxies which we can
see today must have been sent on their way over 6,000 million
years ago! Nevertheless, this word "beginning" is the first
significant word in the first sentence of the Bible. There it
stands like an entrance-gate to Holy Writ. It must surely have
been put there to give us access to the proper understanding
of the whole Bible.

All God's dealings since the beginning of creation have
been concerned solely with man's salvation. God plans that
man's salvation shall be effected in historic time. The word
"beginning" connotes time. Moreover, when the Bible says
that God created the world in six days, it indicates that the
event of creation took place in time. The account of creation
may not be a historical account in the modern sense, but we
can nonetheless perceive in it the historical outlook which is
in evidence throughout all Holy Writ. We often find the
Bible dating events of sacred history, such as, for example,

the calling and activities of the Prophets (Hos. i.1; Isa. vi.1), Israel's deliverance from the Babylonian Captivity (2 Chron. xxxvi. 22f.; Ezra i.1–3), the birth of Jesus (Luke ii.1f.), the appearance of John the Baptist (Luke iii.1f.). Care is always taken to emphasize that God's work for our salvation did not take place in the mists of hoary antiquity, but in the clear light of history. God's work for man's salvation is a historical work. Man's salvation is effected in the course of history, in a particular place and at a particular time.

God's work for creation, for mankind, for each of us, is performed in historic time. We all experience his saving power in some place and at some time. We attach great importance to establishing the place and date of a person's birth and of his death. These are two fixed historical points, and between them lies the single, non-recurring historical event which is that person's life. The clearly defined span of historical time that constitutes the life of any man is the time for that man's salvation, the time when God offers him the chance of salvation; but it is also the time when that man can, and should, seize the opportunity of salvation that God holds out to him. For God can only effect man's salvation if man does his part during his time on earth.

We must now return, however, to the question of our approach to the biblical statement that God created the world in *six days*. We took this as indicating the temporal and historical nature of the process of creation. We can also see at once that this way of presenting his subject enables the sacred writer to depict creation as proceeding in a perfectly smooth and orderly manner to its conclusion. He wants to draw attention to the fact that God went about his work with a definite plan in mind. As the external frame of his plan God chooses the week. The week was the frame into which the normal life of the ancient Israelites was fitted; it continues, indeed, to regulate our own lives in the western world. Biblical man was very much impressed by the order and arrangement he saw in God's creation, but we can be sure he was no more impressed than we are. Today, naturally, we know much more than the Hebrews of old about the laws God imposed on nature. Man in our time, as never before, is master of creation; he can cross the Atlantic in a few hours, he can rocket into space, he has even managed to put off death for a decade or so longer (on the average) than his not-too-remote ancestors. But all this has not come about because man has imposed new laws on creation, but because he has succeeded in discovering some of the most recondite laws that God has inserted in creation.

We also know, however, that there is a twofold order in creation—the cosmic order and the moral order. The cosmic order is independent of our will; the sun rises in the morning and sets in the evening whether we like it or not. But the moral order is given into our own hands. If God were to abrogate the laws of nature, creation would fall back into chaos. If we were to abrogate the moral order, chaos would take possession of human society, of the family, of our own hearts. The question, "How do I stand in relation to God?" is no mere abstraction; we can now realize its full concrete significance. "Have I, a creature, fitted myself into the order of creation, as I should have done; or is there chaos in my life and in my heart?" If I am in chaos, then I am unfortunate indeed and I should lose no time in bringing order into my chaos.

The account of creation takes cognizance not only of God's

activity during his six-day working-week but also of his rest on the seventh day. Holy Writ does not, of course, imply that God needed rest after his work, and that his activity was followed by inactivity. In God the most intense activity coexists with the most complete repose. In the words of St. Augustine, "You, Lord, are ever in action and ever at rest" (*Conf.* 13, 37). But human limitations ordain that we can only accomplish in successive spells what God performs uninterruptedly. We are called upon to do the work that God has given us, in the span of life he has allotted us (our "six days" of work), and, having done our work well, as well as we can, to enter then into God's rest. "But the seventh day is without evening. It has no sunset. After all your works, which were very good, you rested on the seventh day—although you made them with no interruption of your repose. And likewise the voice of your book tells us that we also, after our works— which are only very good because you have granted us to accomplish them—will rest in you in the Sabbath of life everlasting." It is St. Augustine speaking again (*Conf.* 13, 36), and the everlasting Sabbath he speaks of is that which is attested by Holy Writ: "A Sabbath rest, therefore, is reserved for the people of God (Heb. iv.9).

2 God Created Man in His Own Image

Then God said, "Let us make man in our image, after our likeness; and let them have dominion over the fish of the sea, and over the birds of the air, and over the cattle, and over all the earth, and over every creeping thing that creeps upon the earth."

So God created man in his own image, in the image of God he created him; male and female he created them.

And God blessed them, and God said to them, "Be fruitful and multiply, and fill the earth and subdue it; and have dominion over the fish of the sea and over the birds of the air and over every living thing that moves upon the earth."

And God said, "Behold, I have given you every plant yielding seed which is upon the face of all the earth, and every tree with seed in its fruit; you shall have them for food. And to every beast of the earth, and to every bird of the air and to everything that creeps on the earth, everything that has the breath of life, I have given every green plant for food." And it was so (Gen. i.26–30).

We have seen, in the biblical account of creation, how man was created last of all. On this point, at any rate, the Bible and modern science happen to agree. But we saw, too, that the Bible does not set out to teach us anthropology. Yet, in spite of the sensational findings of scientists during the past few decades, there are still people who will go to great trouble to try and prove that the letter of the Bible and the findings of science are in complete harmony. Such efforts are misplaced, because the Bible has no pretensions to be scientific. What the Bible says binds us only insofar as it professes to be doctrine bearing on man's salvation. If, therefore, the biblical account of creation says that man was created last of all, that is no reason for believing he was created last in order of time, last in order of arrival on earth; the Bible means rather that man was created last in logical order, last and greatest in order of worth. The whole of the creation narrative is built up from the bottom, and the object is to show that man, the last to be created, *stands above all other crea-tures and that God alone is above him.*

In our first chapter we touched on the question whether man's place in the modern world has changed. His mastery of the forces of nature is to all appearances, greater than ever. But surely that is the place the Bible assigns to him—do-minion over all creation: "Fill the earth and subdue it; have dominion over the fish of the sea and over the birds of the air and over everything that moves upon the earth." The words we usually translate as "subdue it" have a quite excep-tional force in the original Hebrew. Their literal meaning is "trample it under foot." Man is to behave in such a manner as to leave no doubt that he is lord of creation. We have every reason to be astonished that so much has been given into man's hands. The ancient Israelites themselves showed their astonishment in the eighth psalm:

What is man that thou art mindful of him and the son
of man that thou dost care for him?
Yet thou hast made him a little less than God, and
dost crown him with glory and honor . . .
Thou hast put all things under his feet.

We know now that the sun and the Milky Way are not unique of their kind. There are thousands of millions of milky ways or galaxies, and each is made up of thousands of millions of suns, and each of these suns has its own solar sys-tem (not, as a rule, visible to us). Nonetheless, Holy Writ rings truer than ever when it says of man

Thou hast made him a little less than God . . .
Thou hast put all things under his feet.

We know, of course, that all man's discoveries can never make him a creator. Man does not create, he only discovers, and turns to account, the forces that God has invested in creation. We certainly owe it to man's ingenuity that electric light enables me to write, and you to read, these lines, but nevertheless we owe the light to forces that God has implanted in creation; man has discovered and utilized them. Today we are familiar with natural forces undreamt of by earlier generations, and we can be sure that later generations will be familiar with forces that we cannot even imagine. The discovery in nature of a hitherto unknown force is a stupendous experience for the discoverer. I knew one such man who was overcome with emotion whenever he began to speak of his discovery. Man's efforts to extend his control over the cosmos are not inspired by the powers of evil. Even when man tries, as he does today, to reach the moon, it is not the prince of darkness that urges him on; man is simply fulfilling God's charge to him to bring all creation under his sway. We are not to think that, in consequence of all this, man is going to become bigger and God smaller. Man will certainly become bigger, but God will be bigger still. Even if we were to succeed in producing new life by artificial means—and by all accounts we are not very far from it—such life would be *only life from God's life*.

How is it that man's place in the cosmos is unique? The Bible gives us the answer to this question too:

> *God created man in his own image,*
> *in the image of God he created him.*

What a daring thing to say! Man is God's image! But our sacred writer is in the habit of weighing his words carefully.

He must surely have realized the audacity of this statement. Of no other creature did he say that it was God's image. How, then, did he come to say it of man?

Because no other creature is said to be God's image, and because man is distinct from other creatures in that he has a soul and a mind, we usually say that man is God's image through possessing these spiritual qualities. This is true, so far as it goes, but it does not go far enough. Hebrew thought does not make the same metaphysical distinction between soul and body as western thought does. The ancient Israelites looked at man in the round—as a whole and undivided being. The very idea "image" implies that he was thought of as something *visible and tangible*. But man is only visible and tangible through the medium of his body. The sacred writer marvels at the harmony and beauty of the human body and sees in it a visible and tangible image of the harmony and beauty of God. In the human mind, so to speak, God takes human shape. The more we make this biblical approach our own, the better. The thought that our neighbor's body and our own are made to God's image will give us the proper attitude of reverence towards both of them and will remind us, too, that we have certain duties in their regard: we must care for them and keep them in good health, but we must also train and discipline them.

The sacred writer, certainly, was not preoccupied with the body only, or with the spirit (soul and mind) only, but with body and spirit together, with the whole man, in fact. This old Hebrew author knew quite well that what distinguishes man from the animals was not so much the greater beauty of his physique as his spiritual qualities of soul and mind (cf. Gen. ii.19f). The sacred writer knew also that man's body acquires its dignity and its most enduring beauty from his spiritual nature. And it is precisely this knowledge of the inter-action of spirit and body that makes the Bible refrain from contrasting them—or indeed treating them as mutual. ene-mies, as Plato's philosophy did by representing the body to be the prison of the soul. The ancient Israelites had a remark-ably strong sense of the vitality of the human body—a charac-teristic which seems still to persist in the Jewish people. So far as the Bible is concerned, it is not the soul that lives, but the *person*, the whole human being. The whole of man's physical make-up has God's seal upon it, the seal of his creative power, of his beauty. All the powers, but all the weak-nesses, too, of man's human nature, have been willed and blessed by God. This comprehensive, undivided view of man's nature is a prerequisite for the proper understanding of the Christian doctrine of the Redemption. As God created man's body and his human nature, so also does he redeem man's body and his human nature. At Mass we say, "O God, by whom the dignity of human nature was wondrously estab-lished and yet more wonderfully restored." Our own genera-tion appears to have acquired a new understanding of this integral way of looking at man's nature. We now think that Christ may want something more of man than the sanctifica-tion and salvation of his "immortal soul." For Christ has not redeemed the soul, but the whole man, and our pattern of Christian perfection cannot be the "angelic soul"; it must be the redeemed man. It cannot be the purged and sanctified *soul*; it must be the purged and sanctified man. Our ultimate hope, also, is not the "immortality of the soul," but the resur-rection of the body. Today, as always, the Christian Church concludes its creed not with the words, "I believe in the immortality of the soul," but with the words, "I believe in the resurrection of the body and life everlasting."

Man, being a compound of the spiritual and the corporal, stands midway between God and the world. God is above him and the world is beneath him. Does he belong more to one than the other? We must certainly take the Bible's word for it and the Bible says that man belongs more to God. That is what the Bible means when it calls man "God's image." And here again we feel that the Bible sees man's likeness to God not only in his physical characteristics but in his spiritual qualities, his qualities of soul and mind. By virtue of his soul and mind man is lord of creation. God provides him with food and drink, for the nourishment and refreshment of his body, but he is only true to his human dignity when he obeys the warnings of his soul and mind and is temperate in their use. The animals, also, are there primarily for his bodily needs, but he is only true to his human dignity when he dominates them by his spiritual qualities. Anyone who knows how to handle animals is well aware that animals are trained more by man's will—by his soul and mind—than by man's whip. Animals have no soul or mind, but they sense the gulf between them and man. Man often seems to forget that he has these spiritual qualities, and then he behaves like an animal. He would do well to remember that no animal can fill the place of friend or child or spouse.

God, therefore, has placed all creation under the dominion of man. But over one creature, and only one, God has given him no dominion, and that creature is man's fellow man. No human being may ever exercise absolute power over another. Only God has absolute dominion over mankind. In this way God has pronounced judgment on all tyrants, on the great tyrants of history and on the petty tyrants we meet every day who make the lives of others a veritable hell. We all know the tyrannies that husband can exercise over wife, brother over sister, mother over daughter, mother superior over the sisters in her charge, a worker over his colleagues, a lover over his beloved. On all these tyrannies the Bible pronounces judgment, because our fellow men have also been created in God's image, in freedom of soul and mind.

There are, of course, legitimate forms of earthly authority which decide, within their proper sphere, who is to command and who to obey. But such authority exists only for the purpose of concerting human efforts in an orderly and reasonable manner. Nothing worth while could ever come of any business in which everyone did as he pleased, and this certainly applies with added force to Army, State and Church. Here again, however, a superior may give his subordinates only lawful commands; he has no right to domineer over them.

And with that we come to man's besetting temptation—to let himself be dominated by things that he should dominate, by food and drink, by a car, by money, by work, by knowledge, and to dominate or domineer where he should not, that is, over his neighbor. "But you are not to be called rabbi," says our Lord in Matt. xxiii.8, "for you have one teacher, and you are all brethren."

3 Male and Female He Created

In the day that the Lord God made the earth and the heavens, when no plant of the field was yet in the earth and no herb of the field had yet sprung up—for the Lord God had not caused it to rain upon the earth, and there was no man to till the ground; but a mist went up from the earth and watered the whole face of the ground—then the Lord God formed man of dust from the ground, and breathed into his nostrils the breath of life; and man became a living being . . . Then the Lord God said, "It is not good that man should be alone; I will make him a helper fit for him." So out of the ground the Lord God formed every beast of the field and every bird of the air, and brought them to the man to see what he would call them; and whatever the man called every living creature, that was its name. The man gave names to all cattle, and to the birds of the air, and to every beast of the field; but for the man there was not found a helper fit for him. So the Lord God caused a deep sleep to fall upon the man, and while he slept took one of his ribs and closed up its place with flesh; and the rib which the Lord God had taken from the man he made into a woman and brought her to the man. Then the man said,

> This at last is bone of my bones and flesh of my flesh;
> she shall be called Woman,
> because she was taken out of Man.

Therefore a man leaves his father and his mother and cleaves to his wife, and they become one flesh (Gen. ii.4–7, 18–24).

Finally, brethren, we beseech and exhort you in the Lord Jesus, that as you learned from us how you ought to live and

to please God, just as you are doing, you do so more and
more. For you know what instructions we gave you through
the Lord Jesus. For this is the will of God, your sanctification:
that you abstain from immorality; that each one of you know
how to take a wife for himself in holiness and honor, not in
the passion of lust like heathen who do not know God; that
no man transgress, and defraud his brother in business, because the Lord is an avenger in all these things, as we sol-
emnly forewarned you. For God has not called us for unclean-
ness, but in holiness (1 Thess. iv.1–7).

We have already considered the account of the creation of
man and woman which forms part of the story of God's six
days of creation and fills the first chapter of the Book of
Genesis; it told us that God created man in his own image.
The passage from the second chapter of Genesis which we
have quoted above gave us an entirely different account of
the same event. At the time when these first chapters of
Genesis were written, various traditions about the origins of
mankind were current in Israel. The account of creation in
the first chapter of Genesis was the work of a learned theo-
logian. His reference to the ticklish subject of man's creation
could not be more restrained. The precise manner of man's
origin was then, as now, a particularly resistant problem. So
the learned and inspired writer of the first chapter of the
Bible will not commit himself on how God created man; he
concerns himself only with what man is, and he tells us man
is created in God's image. But other religious teachers in
ancient Israel were less self-conscious in their treatment of
popular traditions about man's creation. It was one of these

that was responsible for the account of this event in the second chapter of Genesis. He gives a vivid, picturesque, and detailed description of it. In this figurative language he clothes the substance of his doctrine. We must not stop short at the picturesque garb in which he presents his teaching; we must strip it off to get at the doctrine underneath. When, therefore, the sacred writer tells us that God formed man of dust from the ground and breathed into his nostrils the breath of life, we can take him to mean that man is as frail as an earthenware vessel, but the divine breath of life is in him nevertheless: he has received life from God's life.

The Bible, accordingly, is here concerned not with *how* man originated, but with *what* man is. The sacred writer is preoccupied with the question we put to ourselves at the beginning of this book: *What is the relationship between God and man?* We said then that the Bible gives us the answer to *this* question. But we can draw no conclusions from the Bible as to *how* God created the human body. Up to about a hundred years ago it was generally assumed that God created the human body in the form in which it is familiar to us all. Today, however, we may legitimately hold that man's body, as we know it, and all animal life in common with it, are the results of a very long process of evolution. Neither the old theory nor the new one can look to the Bible for support, for the simple reason that the problem does not fall within its cognizance. It is a scientific, and not a theological, problem, and God did not purport to throw any light upon it because it has no bearing on man's salvation. But let us never think that by accepting the theory of evolution we derogate in the slightest from God's greatness! Surely God must be all the greater for investing a primitive life with the power to evolve through hundreds of millions of years into what the sacred writer calls, with superb insight, *God's image.*

The creation of the woman out of a part of the man's body must also be treated as a picturesque presentation of doctrine. Here, too, it is plain that the Bible does not profess to tell us *how* God created the woman; if the man's body is the end-product of a long process of evolution, the woman's body must have taken the same course. The Bible shows us, instead, *what* woman is; she is the natural helpmate of man, but her relationship to man is also, to some extent, one of dependence. That is what St. Paul means when he says, "The husband is the head of the wife" (Eph. v.23). At the same time, the biblical narrative teaches us that marriage is the lawful and indissoluble union of one man with one woman and explains why married love is the highest kind of earthly love.

Now that we have grasped these points, let us turn back to the text we started from: "God created man in his own image." We have already tried to puzzle out what this means. The same verse, however (Gen. i.27), concludes with the words, "male and female he created them." What a curious thing for the Bible to say! Certainly we should never have known that man was God's image if the Bible had not said so. But it hardly requires a divinely inspired biblical text to assure us that there are men and women in the world; every child knows that. All the same, it is unthinkable that the concluding phrase of Gen. i.27 can be a deliberate banality. By saying categorically that God created man male and female, the Bible surely means to anticipate questions that may give us furiously to think! The very last thing the Bible says about the event of creation is that God created man male and female. Man and woman are the last to be created; man and woman are, somehow or other, the quintessence, the most perfect product, of all creation. We often find it irritating that man and woman are the pivots on which everything in this world turns. But we have the Bible's authority for it. To put it plainly, man and woman are the whole world or, inversely, the whole world is man and woman.

Now, if the Bible says in the same breath that God created man in his own image and that he created man male and female, there must surely be an intrinsic connection between these two statements, and that connection must be that man can only be God's image when he is man and woman. We have seen already what a risky thing it was for God to make man in his own image or, indeed, for him to create an image of himself at all. Can there ever be an image of God? God is infinite and knows no bounds; a creature is always finite and limited. How, then, can a creature capture and reflect all the perfection of God? In God the greatest contrasts are to be found in juxtaposition. Just and merciful, powerful and tender, his are the sun's fire and the rose's fragrance. How could God pour all his abundance into a single vessel? It would seem as if he shared it between two vessels—one for his justice and power, the other for his mercy and tenderness.

This must not be misunderstood or twisted to mean that man is only one-half of God's image, and woman only the other half. Both are created in God's image, but each in the way that is most fitting. Moreover, there are divine qualities —God's wisdom, for example, and his faithfulness—that must be common to man and woman. The woman, indeed, must possess some of the so-called masculine attributes, and the man some of those usually considered to be womanly. Woman must be capable of courage (and how often is she braver than man!) and man must be capable of tenderness (and his heart is often softer than hers). A distinguished woman of our time, Ottilie Mosshamer, once wrote: "A man who is only masculine is an intolerable bore, and a woman who is only feminine is an insufferable ninny."

Unmarried persons run the danger of being incomplete. God has made the sexes complementary, one supplying the other's deficiencies. It is to their advantage to cooperate in the tasks he has assigned them.

We can also see why maintaining right relations between man and woman is so important, and yet so difficult. But then things that are worth while must always be difficult and things that cost nothing are worth nothing. At the head of this chapter we quoted a passage from St. Paul's first letter to the Thessalonians. God, he wrote, has charged every man to be holy. And what must a man do to be holy? We are amazed at St. Paul's simple recipe. A man, he says, should not defraud another in business and he should treat his wife with respect. And the New Testament actually began with the letter which contains this recipe for holiness, for St. Paul's first letter to the Thessalonians was the first portion of the New Testament to be written. Nobody would maintain that the two demands in this recipe are impossible ones; so nobody can maintain that it is impossible to become holy.

Holiness, therefore, means that a husband must treat his wife with respect. The measure of a man's moral greatness is his behavior to his wife, and the measure of a woman's greatness is her behavior to her husband. Whoever proves equal to this requirement will prove equal to life's other tasks. Let us, therefore, here and now, accept the charge that God gives us to be holy, and let us fulfil it as God would have us do. If we do that, we need not fear to face the question, "How do I stand in relation to God?"

4 So when the Woman Saw that the Tree Was Good for Food . . .

And the Lord God planted a garden in Eden, in the east; and there he put the man whom he had formed. And out of the ground the Lord God made to grow every tree that is pleasant to the sight and good for food, the tree of life also in the midst of the garden, and the tree of the knowledge of good and evil . . . And the Lord God commanded the man, saying, "You may freely eat of every tree of the garden; but of the tree of the knowledge of good and evil you shall not eat, for in the day that you eat of it you shall die."

Now the serpent was more subtle than any other wild creature that the Lord God had made. He said to the woman, "Did God say 'You shall not eat of any tree of the garden?' " and the woman said to the serpent, "We may eat of the fruit of the trees of the garden; but God said, 'You shall not eat of the fruit of the tree which is in the midst of the garden, neither shall you touch it, lest you die.' " But the serpent said to the woman, "You will not die. For God knows that when you eat of it your eyes will be opened, and you will be like God, knowing good and evil." So when the woman saw that the tree was good for food, and that it was a delight to the eyes, and that the tree was to be desired to make one wise, she took of its fruit and ate; and she also gave some to her husband, and he ate. Then the eyes of both were opened, and they knew that they were naked; and they sewed fig leaves together and made themselves aprons.

And they heard the sound of the Lord God walking in the garden in the cool of the day, and the man and his wife hid themselves from the presence of the Lord God among the trees of the garden. But the Lord God called to the man and said to him, "Where are you?" And he said, "I heard the sound of thee in the garden, and I was afraid, because I was naked; and I hid myself." He said, "Who told you that you were naked? Have you eaten of the tree of which I commanded you not to eat?" The man said, "The woman whom thou gavest to be with me, she gave me fruit of the tree, and I ate." Then the Lord God said to the woman, "What is this that you have done?" The woman said, "The serpent beguiled me, and I ate" (Gen. ii.8f., 16f.; iii.1–13).

Another parable he put before them, saying, "The kingdom of heaven may be compared to a man who sowed good seed in his field; but while men were sleeping, his enemy came and sowed weeds among the wheat, and went away. So when the plants came up and bore grain, then the weeds appeared also. And the servants of the householder came and said to him, 'Sir, did you not sow good seed in your field? How then has it weeds?' He said to them, 'An enemy has done this'" (Matt. xiii.24–8).

To understand the paradise narrative also, we must have regard to the figurative way in which it is presented. We should not, of course, take it literally and suppose that God actually planted a garden and placed the first human couple in it—or, indeed, that the first members of the human race ever lived in a well-tended garden. We can rest assured that mankind, from its first appearance on this earth had to contend with all the hardships of human existence. Nevertheless, God was a good father to primitive man. He had equipped him with everything necessary for survival. Man was well provided for. In particular, God had given him the intelligence that would enable him to prevail over the rigors of nature. In the various ice ages through which Europe passed, the primitive animals had to flee to warmer regions; those that could not, died out. But man survived, in spite of temperatures of 50 degrees centigrade or so below zero. He survived because of the intelligence that made him superior to the animals and —what is more to the point—taught him the art of fire-making.

There is much more than this, however, in the typology of the paradise garden. A closer look at it shows us that God also lives in the garden; he and man live there in company. The sacred writer uses the image of the garden to tell us that man originally lived in close proximity to God and in God's friendship. And this makes the meaning of man's expulsion from the garden all too plain: henceforward man was no longer to live in God's company; he had forfeited God's friendship.

If the garden cannot be taken literally, neither can the forbidden tree and its fruit. The description, "tree of the knowledge of good and evil," is typically Semitic. Although we now have a very good knowledge of the modes of thought and expression of the ancient Semites, we have not yet succeeded in finding a completely satisfactory explanation of why the forbidden tree is called the "tree of the knowledge of good and evil." But this does not really matter very much because what it stands for is absolutely clear. God has been a good father to man and has given him everything necessary for his welfare. True, God has not given him *everything*, no more than the best of fathers would give everything to a child of his. But man was not content with what God had given him. He must needs hanker after what God had not given him. What a poor view he took of God's love for him! He was under the delusion that he could attain perfect happiness only if he got what God had not given him. God, he thinks, has withheld it from him because God grudges him his happiness. And so, man reached out after this imaginary happiness only to find that he had brought real and grievous unhappiness upon himself instead.

The nice psychological judgment of the inspired author in his story of man's fall still evokes our admiration. We can only say that he must have been a man with a keen insight into the problem of life and the working of the human heart. And neither of these has changed in the slightest since he first told his story some three thousand years ago. The forbidden tree had not troubled the woman at all until the serpent appeared on the scene, and her unconcern had preserved her from temptation. But once the serpent had succeeded in bringing the tree to her notice and focussing her attention on it, the woman was lost. "So when the woman saw that the tree was good for food and that it was a delight to the eyes, she took of its fruit and ate." The sin was committed almost before she had moved a step nearer the tree. Which of us has not already found to his cost that when he took the first seemingly innocuous step on the downward slope, he per-

suaded himself he had done nothing wrong? Which of us
could have suspected at the time that he had broken down
the barriers and cleared the way for sin? Had the woman
done wrong already by looking at the tree? Surely God had
not forbidden her to look at it! And yet, when she did so, her
fate was sealed.

It is hard to explain man's strange conduct in so lightly for-
getting all the good things God has given him and in per-
suading himself that he can never be happy until he gets
hold of some useless object on which he has set his heart. All
too late he learns the truth, and how bitter it is! The serpent
had promised heaven and earth. You will be like God"—
nothing less! But the reality turned out to be pitifully human: "They knew that they were naked." The fruits of the
sin were nakedness, privation, and shame. Man's fanciful
castle in the air collapsed like a bubble and left behind an
indelible blot of shame. Even when our sin is seen by nobody, we feel we have cause to be ashamed before the whole
world, and we see the whole world pointing the finger of
scorn at us. Theology has a word for it, and a most apt word
it is—the mystery of sin. Sin is a mystery; there is an element
in it that cannot be gauged by merely human standards. Let
us go back over something we said in a previous chapter.
Man is lord over all creation, but so is his fellow man who
stands beside him on the same level; above man there is God,
who is lord over man. No man, therefore, is given an entirely
free hand vis-à-vis the whole of creation. Limits have been set
to man's lordship to ensure that his fellow man shall be beside him and not under him. I have my place in life; and my
fellow man has his, and I have neither dominion over it nor
the right to trespass on it with impunity. Every man, then, is

answerable to God, who is above him, and to his fellow man, who is beside him. If we go through the Ten Commandments we find that none of them says anything as to what our attitude should be toward *the rest of creation*; man has a free hand here because the rest of creation is subject to him. The Commandments are all concerned with the relations between man and God, and man and his neighbor, and in neither of these spheres is man given *carte blanche*. The obligations that God lays on man are not just divine caprices to irritate and embitter him or—as the serpent insinuated in our story —to withhold the full measure of his happiness from him. On the contrary, these obligations are expressly designed to ensure man's lasting happiness. Over all mankind reigns God, our loving Father, whose will to save us knows no bounds. Man, however, can only be truly happy when he fulfils certain obligations. If everybody were to drive as he pleased on the public highway, keeping to the right or the left as the fancy took him, nobody would be happy, and the accident rate would be stupendous. But accidents would be avoided if a definite highway code were instituted and if everybody observed it. Mankind, too, brings untold evils upon itself because it does not observe the code God has given it.

But why is man so foolish as to prefer evil to good? Here we come upon the mystery that baffles the human mind. The story of paradise gives us an insight into this mystery. The serpent is only a figure, a symbol of a monstrous power, of Satan, the adversary who thrusts himself between God and man. God strives unceasingly to raise up a holy people for himself, but Satan does all he can to make the holy people unholy. God is that householder in the parable who sowed only good seed in his field; yet, when the plants came up, a

great growth of weeds was among them. His servants, astonished, asked him, "Did you not sow good seed in your field?
How then has it weeds?" But the master showed no surprise.
"An enemy," he said, "has done this." And that enemy has a
powerful influence upon man. But it is beyond his powers to
compel man to commit sin. Man is a free agent. The paradise
narrative tells us plainly that, while the serpent instigates the
sin, man is the guilty one and knows it.

It should have dawned on us by now that the real purpose
of the biblical story of the Fall is not to record the very first
sin committed by mankind, but to describe sin in general,
the sins of all of us. We are inclined to treat the Bible story
much too lightly. When some fresh disorder arises in our dis-
tracted world, somebody is sure to complain, "See what
Adam and Eve have brought upon us!" (Or, if we do not express that sentiment, we feel it.) If, however, we want to be
honest with ourselves, we have to acknowledge that the sin
of Adam and Eve is not responsible for the world's disorder
today. Our present ills are not caused by the sins of the past,
but by the sins of the present. We must admit also that the
disorder in our own lives is not due to the sin of Adam and
Eve, but to our own sins. The lesson of the Fall is that, in
the long run, man need fear only *one* misfortune, and that
is sin.

We should not, then, look upon the paradise narrative as
merely an account of an isolated historical fact recorded for
our information. We fail to understand the story of Adam
and Eve if we fail to recognize ourselves in them. Let us go
back over our sins, sins we thought at the time would bring
us happiness and only lost us God instead, and with him
everything. When we have done this, let us ask ourselves

honestly whether any of these sins has made us the least bit happier.

The Old Testament sees mankind sunk deep in the mire of sin. The Prophets take a pessimistic view of man's condition. Humanly speaking, there would seem to be no salvation possible for their people; sin has become second nature with them. In the words of Jeremiah:

> *Can the Ethiopian change his skin*
> *or the leopard his spots?*
> *Then also you can do good*
> *who are accustomed to do evil.*
> —(*Jer. xiii.23*)

And so it is. We can all commit sin, and we do. But only One can take away sin, and he does. In him we shall find *forgiveness and mercy beyond measure* (cf. 2 Sam. xxiv.14; Ps. cxxx).

5 *I Will Put Enmity Between You and the Woman*

The Lord God said to the serpent,

> *Because you have done this,*
>   *cursed are you above all cattle,*
>   *and above all wild animals;*
> *upon your belly you shall go,*
>   *and dust you shall eat*
>   *all the days of your life.*

I will put enmity between you and the
   woman,
      and between your seed and her seed;
   he shall bruise your head,
      and you shall bruise his heel.

To the woman he said,

I will greatly multiply your pain in
   childbearing;
      in pain you shall bring forth children,
      yet your desire shall be for your
         husband,
      and he shall rule over you.

And to Adam he said,

Because you have listened to the voice
   of your wife,
      and have eaten of the tree
      of which I commanded you,
      "You shall not eat of it,"
   cursed is the ground because of you;
      in toil you shall eat of it all the
         days of your life;
   thorns and thistles it shall bring forth to
      you;
      and you shall eat the plants of the
         field.
   In the sweat of your face
      you shall eat bread
   till you return to the ground,

> for out of it you were taken;
>   you are dust,
>   and to dust you shall return.
>   —(Gen. iii.14–19.)

If the world hates you, know that it has hated me before it hated you. If you were of the world, the world would love its own; but because you are not of the world, but I chose you out of the world, therefore the world hates you. Remember the word that I said to you, "A servant is not greater than his master." If they persecuted me, they will persecute you; if they kept my word, they will keep yours also. But all this they will do to you on my account, because they do not know him who sent me. If I had not come and spoken to them, they would not have sin; but now they have no excuse for their sin. He who hates me hates my Father also. If I had not done among them the works which no one else did, they would not have sin, but now they have seen and hated both me and my Father. It is to fulfil the word that is written in their law, "They hated me without a cause" (John xv.18–25).

After the Fall, God pronounced judgment on each of the three participants individually. The serpent was condemned henceforth to creep on its belly and eat dust; moreover, there would exist a state of enmity between it and mankind. The woman was to bear her children in pain. The man was to labor on the land—and eventually die.

It is obvious that this passage can no more be taken literally than the passages that told us of God's six-day working week and the details of man's creation. The divine judgments (Gen. iii.14–19) belong to the same literary mode as the whole of the paradise narrative and must be interpreted on the same principles. The judgments have no relevance to physical science and the course it took. From what we know of nature's laws, the serpent has crept on its belly from time immemorial and not merely from the time of man's first sin. From time immemorial, too, woman's childbearing has been accompanied by the pangs of birth, and man has labored on the land and eventually died. We saw, however, in our first chapter how God instituted in his creation a physical (or cosmic) order and a moral order. It is with the latter that Holy Writ is concerned. As the account of creation does not state categorically that sin brought about any disturbance of the physical order, we may very well infer from the paradise narrative that the disturbance took place in the moral order. We know our sacred writer well enough by this to realize that it is his habit to convey fundamental spiritual truths by means of the homely imagery of everyday life. He depicts the moral disorder produced by sin as if it were a disturbance of the physical order. When the sacred writer tells us that God condemned man to death after the Fall, he means to convey something more serious and more profound than a superficial reading and a literal interpretation would lead us to expect. There is a worse death than physical death—the death that is the result of sin. It is that sort of death that really spells disaster. Physical death persists as an element in the new order of salvation instituted by Jesus Christ. But Jesus has done away with the death that comes through sin, the death that is an unmitigated evil. For Jesus is "the Lamb of God, who takes away the sin of the world" (John i.29).

Sin came about because man made a pact with the serpent. To break the power of sin, Jesus must break up the alliance and force the two allies apart. Therein lies the significance of the Gospel accounts of the casting out of devils. Jesus has to deal not only with the saving of a poor, possessed soul, but with a demoniacal attack on the very structure of creation; man's pact with the serpent has to be broken, both partners separated, and the ground between them rent asunder in order that a chasm may divide them. Satan's rule is replaced by God's rule. "If it is by the finger of God that I cast out demons," said Jesus on one such occasion, "then the kingdom of God has come upon you" (Luke xi.20). God's rule and Satan's rule are incompatible. That is also the lesson we learn from the Gospel passages (Matt. iv.1–11; Luke iv.1–13) which describe how Jesus allowed Satan to tempt him as he was about to begin his messianic mission. When Jesus curtly repulses Satan's three temptations, he gives us to understand that we cannot serve both God and Satan; we have to opt for one or the other. "No man," Jesus says elsewhere, "can serve two masters" (Matt. vi.24).

We can now grasp the meaning of the judgment God pronounced on the serpent. God said, "I will put enmity between you and the woman, and between your seed and her seed; he shall bruise your head, and you shall bruise his heel." The outcome of this struggle between the serpent's seed and the woman's seed was by no means clear in the context of the Old Covenant. But the Christian faith clarifies the issue. The Apocalypse of St. John, in a passage which obviously refers to the Genesis text we are discussing, describes the course and the issue of this life-and-death struggle between Christ (between every Christian, indeed, with Christ's help) and the

evil one. The woman is about to bear a child and cries out
in her labor; before her stands the dragon—"that ancient serpent" (Apoc. xx.2)—waiting to devour her child when she
brings it forth. (We can take the woman to represent Israel
about to give birth to the infant Messiah.) The child
(Christ) is "caught up to God and to his throne"; but on
earth the fight goes on between the dragon and the rest of
the woman's offspring who keep the commandments of God
and bear testimony to Jesus (Apoc. xii.2, 4, 5, 17). As God's
plan of salvation has been continued, through Christ, by a
new covenant, we may now regard the woman as personifying
God's people under the New Testament—that is, the Church.

This, then, is the explanation that the last book of Holy
Writ gives of the "enmity" passage in the first book. Never
again must there be friendship between man and the serpent, between man and the evil one. Man must choose between the friendship of God and the friendship of Satan. A
passage in the New Testament reads, "Whoever wishes to be
a friend of the world, makes himself an enemy of God" (Jas.
iv.4). But the friend of God draws on himself the hatred of
the world. All the descendants of Eve, all mankind down the
ages, are called on to declare war on the serpent, to take up
arms against the adversary. In his last discourse to the disciples, Jesus spoke not only of the love he bore them, but also
—and with even more emphasis—of the hatred the world
bears for his Father, for himself and for his disciples (John
xv.9–24). Elsewhere, too, he says he has not come to bring
peace, but a sword (Matt. x.34; cf. Luke xxii.36), and that
the Scripture must be fulfilled in him (Luke xxii.36–7).
Death and evil are with us still, but that is no reason why we
should add our voices to the doleful chorus of the many who
lament the wickedness of the world, the perversity of man-

kind, and the cumulative evils that press upon us all. Let us look around us at nature, at the sun that never fails to rise, at spring's annual victory over autumn's decay and winter's death. Evil exists only to be overcome by good (*cf.* Rom. xii.21). Death is there only to be overcome by life. The Hebrews of old believed that, at the beginning of time, sorrow, tears and death were unknown. Such an idea must have sprung from a feeling of more substance than a vain sentimental nostalgia. Surely it was a foreshadowing in their souls, by the Holy Spirit, of the "day of the Lord" mentioned by the Prophets, when all these evils would cease to be. The Apocalypse also promises us that when "the former things" have passed away there shall be no more tears or death or mourning or crying or pain or anything accursed (Apoc. xxi.4; xxii.3). And night shall be no more for God's light shall shine on everything (Apoc. xxii.5). The true meaning of the "tree of life" will then be revealed. He who "conquers," he who holds his ground and stays his course in the battle with the serpent—to him it shall be granted to eat of the tree of life which is in the paradise of God, and he shall not be hurt by "the second death." To him, also, it shall be granted to sit with Christ on his throne just as Christ himself—because he has conquered—sits on the Father's right hand (Apoc. ii.7, 11, 17, 26; iii.5, 12, 21).

6 Put on the New Nature

The man called his wife's name Eve, because she was the mother of all living. And the Lord God made for Adam and his wife garments of skins, and clothed them. Then the Lord God said, "Behold, the man has become like one of us, know-

ing good and evil; and now, lest he put forth his hand and
take also of the tree of life, and eat, and live for ever"—therefore the Lord God sent him forth from the garden of Eden,
to till the ground from which he was taken. He drove out the
man; and at the east of the garden of Eden he placed the
cherubim, and a flaming sword which turned every way, to
guard the way to the tree of life (Gen. iii.20–24).

Therefore, if anyone is in Christ, he is a new creation; the
old has passed away, behold, the new has come. All this is
from God, who through Christ reconciled us to himself (2
Cor. v.17f).

So much for the first part of the biblical history of man.
It began full of promise; the first man had come straight
from God's hand; God himself had breathed life into him—
life from his own life. To keep him company God had given
him a wife and the man at first sight of her had cried out in
delight, "This at last is bone of my bones and flesh of my
flesh." A wonderful pair, fresh and lovely as a May morning!
Michelangelo's masterly hand has recaptured the scene in
his painting in the Sistine Chapel: Adam in all his harmony
of body and mind; Eve in the shapeliness and bloom of her
maidenhood. What could we not expect from such a couple!
We read on and in a few minutes see the young couple's
brief spell of happiness shattered into fragments. The dream
of paradise is over; they are turned out into naked reality; and
there the story of Adam and Eve comes to an end.

And yet there are faint gleams of hope in the gloomy
firmament. God had given our first parents clothes to cover
their nakedness—a sign that he would continue to care for

them and had not cast them off altogether. They had hardly left paradise behind them when, we are told, their first child was born (Gen. iv.1). God had left them life, and the power to transmit it. Their dismal end had become a new and auspicious beginning.

And the pendulum continues to swing between end and beginning. Man's growing sinfulness provokes the penalty of the Flood and the human race seems doomed to extermination. But God again gives it a fresh beginning (Gen. 6–9). Nevertheless the new generations lapse into heathenism. (That is the meaning of the Tower of Babel episode in Gen. xi.1–9). Again at the eleventh hour God picks out Abraham to be the founder of a great nation dedicated to his service. But Abraham is childless until he is far advanced in age, and then, against all nature, God gives him a son (Gen. 21). Abraham's posterity are threatened with annihilation during their sojourn in Egypt; it is only at the eleventh hour that God has them rescued by Moses (Exod. 1–3). They are on the point of being driven into the Red Sea when, at the eleventh hour, God leads them safely across. In all these situations, doom and the end seem inevitable, but God never fails to turn the end into a new beginning, each more remarkable than the last. And so the story goes on until the advent of Jesus Christ. At his birth a host of angels sing, but his life peters out in failure, and even his most faithful disciples are left without hope. Yet the stone is no sooner rolled into place before his tomb than an angel comes down from heaven and rolls it back. And to the faithful little band that have come to look for Jesus in the tomb the angel says, "He has risen, he is not here" (Mark xvi.6).

In the life of every Christian, too, there are desperate situations and crucial conjunctures which make him think the end has come, but which actually turn out to be a series of fresh beginnings. These can be blessings in disguise. The schoolboy who has just passed his final examination is delighted to have put his schooldays behind him and to be entering on a new stage of his career. The newly married couple bid farewell to the *existence* they have left and joyfully begin a new *life!* God punctuates our lives with painful crises that, for the moment, seem to be the end of everything—the termination of some work to which we have become attached, the end of a path we had trodden so gaily, the end of a friendship, the end of a love. But when God takes something away from us, he does so only to give us something better in its place, to make us ready for a new task or mission that he has in store for us. God likes to leave us with empty hands so that he can fill them again for us. Whenever we think the end has come, that is just the time when we are due to make a fresh start. As a poet of our own day, Bergengruen, has put it:

> And God still loves the empty hands;
> By losing, we are truly winning.
> And every end turns out to be
> A new and glorious beginning.

After all, what was the Old Covenant but a divinely planned series of new creations? And that is still truer of the New Covenant—its very name tells us so. That is the Covenant sealed with our Savior's resurrection, which ushered in the time of "new heavens and a new earth" (Isa. lxv.17), the time when God is "doing a new thing" (Isa. xliii.19).

With our Lord's resurrection a new era began. And it involved something more than our Lord's rising from the dead and coming back to life, and the fixing of responsibility for his death on those who sent him to the gibbet, and his ultimate and total triumph. All that, of course, is perfectly true, but it is not all. The resurrection of Jesus is an event of cosmic proportions. With his death the old order of creation came to an end, and with his resurrection a new world was born. The first Easter morning saw the birth of a new creation; time made a fresh start. "If anyone is in Christ," says St. Paul, "he is a new creation" (2 Cor. v.17). Strictly speaking, it was man only that was created anew; the hills, the trees, the animal world remained the same as before. But surely all creation must have somehow received new life from the fact that henceforth it would be under the dominion of a mankind that had ceased to be unregenerate and was now redeemed for salvation.

The mission of Jesus was the "new thing" of Isaiah's prophecy. It was designed to be so from the very outset. The first day Jesus appeared in Capharnaum on the shore of the Sea of Galilee, his listeners got the impression that, with him, something really new had burst upon them. "They were astonished at his teaching, for he taught as one who had authority, and not as the scribes . . . They were all amazed, so that they questioned among themselves, saying "What is this? A new teaching?" (Mark i.22, 27). Jesus also makes it plain that whoever would be his disciple must be prepared for a complete break with the old things; he must adopt an entirely new outlook and attitude. "No one," he says, "sews a piece of unshrunk cloth on an old garment; if he does, the patch tears away from it, the new from the old, and a worse tear is made. And no one puts new wine into old wineskins; if he does, the wine will burst the skins, and the wine is lost and so are the skins; but new wine is for fresh skins" (Mark ii.27f). It will not do for the disciple of Jesus to profess a sort of second-class, patched-up Christianity while continuing to lead his old unregenerate life. Christianity is all or nothing; it means being Christian all along the line. And yet, we know only too well how universal is this patched-up Christianity. The main trouble—indeed the tragedy—of Christianity in our so-called Christian countries is that Christians are just as uncharitable, hard-hearted, dishonest and adulterous as heathens—if not more so. But all this has been given a sort of veneer of Christianity—or rather little Christian patches have, so to speak, been inserted all over. Church dues are paid, people go to church on Sundays, there is a certain activity in Christian associations, and there may be a Christian political party. The Gospels give us this lesson of the wine in another characteristic form, as when Jesus says, "And no one after drinking old wine desires new, for he says, 'The old is good' " (Luke v.39). What a good description of the life of the average Christian! He calls himself a follower of Christ, but prefers to stick to the old wine and to let his life go on as before. And yet, Jesus imperatively demands that we shall take up the new life. He calls his commandment of love "the new commandment" (John xiii.34), and the Covenant which he is instituting "the New Covenant" (Luke xxii.20)—the Covenant that is to endure to the end of time. Two thousand years have passed since Jesus inaugurated it, but it is still the New Covenant, and will be 20,000 or 200,000 years hence. Even when his voice was stilled in the silence of death, he let it be seen that a new dispensation had begun: his bruised and torn body was placed in a new tomb in which nobody had yet been laid (Matt. xxvii.60; John xix.41).

Every man henceforth who is called by Christ is, therefore, called to a new life in which his very nature is re-created. St. Paul insists on this with all the emphasis at his command. "Put off your old nature . . . and put on the new nature, created after the likeness of God in true righteousness and holiness" (Eph. iv.22–4). That accounts for the strange tension in the Christian's life; he *is* a new man, and yet his lifelong task is to *become* a new man, to strive to be a new man, to put off his old nature and put on the new. From this we get a much clearer idea of why the Christian's life is so full of difficulties, stress and suffering. These are the instruments that reshape us into new men; and new men cannot be brought forth without travail.

Because Christ presented his message and his work in the guise of a "new thing," true Christianity has always been responsive to new things in all spheres of human endeavor— art, architecture, music, literature, social order, education. Nothing is farther from the Christian spirit than a mentality that is backward-looking on principle; that maintains that our ancestors knew as much as we do; that practises a narrow-minded adherence to tradition and a resolute rejection of every attempted variation on the tried and trusted themes.

Surely the Christian, of all persons, must be open to new things, new ideas. Redeemed humanity is the New Creation. And creation implies development and change. We are more aware than our predecessors that God has made his creation subject to the law of evolution and mutation. We have only to think of the evolution of living creatures from protozoa through ever more complex forms to mammals and, finally,

to man. Just as the first Creation lives under the law of
evolution and change, so does the second, the New Creation.
But the changes to be effected by the New Creation are the
deepening, heightening and broadening of man's spiritual nature so that he may serve God in the most sublime way possible for a human being. This is the task which the risen
Christ has entrusted to his Church. We should have a keen
scent and an alert mind for the changes that he longs to carry
out in his new creation. Only then can we further the work
of him who said, "Behold, I make all things new" (Apoc.
xxi.5).

3 ENCOUNTER WITH GOD

by Gotthold Hasenhüttl

TRANSLATED BY WILLIAM WHITMAN

1 The Failure of Religion

As man's consciousness awakens, he finds that his existence stands open to question. A child will ask, "Why is this man so tall? Why am I going to have a sister? Why does my brother have to die?"

He is not satisfied unless he has answers to these questions, neither now as a child nor later as an adult. And though as a child he still may be satisfied with partial answers, as an adult he can't avoid the fact that his existence is open to question. "How can I find a merciful God?" Luther asked in his great despair. The philosopher questions Existence, asking, "Why am I living? What is the meaning of my life? How will I come to terms with it?" Such questions weigh upon every man, whether he is suffering under their weight or whether, finding no answers, he pushes them aside. In the critical moments in a person's life, when everything threatens to fall apart, when one has nothing left, nothing worth living for, these questions come to the fore again in all their bitterness. And it is then that one looks for something substantial, a refuge where one can flee, be received and be sustained by a loving hand. Is this hand the reality which brings religion to us? Is it God who brings meaning into our existence and allows us to come to terms with life?

This question is as old as the history of mankind. Looking into the past, we encounter thinkers who reply to it in radically different ways. Which of them speaks to the reality in which we are living, which we ourselves make up? Is God an entity we experience in our lives? Does He interest Himself in me and act in my behalf, or must I manage without Him? Might He not possibly even destroy my freedom if I suppose His existence?

Titus Lucretius Carus, the "epicurean" of the first century B.C. and one of Rome's best poets, gives us the oldest complete picture of the atheist's point of view. He maintains that a God who operates in my life and manifests His will in my surroundings can only instill fear, terror and anxiety into me and reduce me to unhappiness. Lucretius wrote six books (De Rerum Natura—On the Nature of Things) in an attempt to give man freedom from the power of God. Even if he doesn't expressly deny the existence of God and gods, their existence is completely meaningless to Lucretius since God or the gods haven't the slightest contact with the world and with men. For everything has its natural cause.

St. Jerome, one of the fathers of the Church, is so staggered by the godlessness of Lucretius' atheistic work that he has Lucretius lose his wits through the drinking of a love-potion and sets his work into a state of mind of lesser or greater madness. According to Jerome, Lucretius' work is supposed to have been left unfinished due to the author's suicide. However, the whole didactic poem radiates a sharp,

logical spirit, and it sounds like the first great destruction of
myth able to offer freedom from religion. Lucretius declares
that the religious man stands before unexplained causes: he is
struck down by sickness; storms lay waste his crops; war and
hunger bring suffering to the people; he is tortured by an
inevitable death wherein he can expect further punishment.
And who is responsible for this punishing? God, answers the
religious man. Who brings about all this sickness and misfortune? Again, God. God's freedom rises up in front of man
and asserts power over him. Man is taken aback before this
unknown God. He sacrifices to Him to obtain appeasement,
but fear continues to weigh upon him.

How may we picture such a man? Isn't he like a child who
is afraid of the dark? With every step he takes, behind every
tree he passes, he sees a face peering out. His steps are anxious
and hesitant, for the path leads into the dark wood and he
can't see where he is going. Such is the man who thinks re-
ligiously and who recognizes God's hand in the events of nature. A beam of sunlight, however bright, cannot help heal a
person of this kind. It cannot remove the darkness from his
soul. Nor can the light of day. Only contemplation of the
light of our intellect can bring this about, our reason.[1] One
should apply himself to the natural laws and to knowledge.
One should bring the principles of all Being to light. Then
fear and anxiety will shrink from the human scene, and man
will be freed from the shackles of religion. "Therefore," says
Lucretius, "I continue to free man's spirit from the fetters
of religion."[2]

However, isn't it still more terrible to have to live without
the hand of God, to have to stop making offerings for his
appeasement, to cease going to the temple where one under-

goes divine experiences? No, the poet answers. Take a sick
person, for example. The doctor has to induce a child to
swallow a bitter absinthe, and if the child resists, thinking it
will do him harm, the medicine has nevertheless been pre-
scribed for his own good and will cause him to recover. And
to make sure the grown child doesn't have too hard a time,
Lucretius continues, I want to mix sweet honey into the
absinthe so that my poetry will be graceful and so the sick
won't balk at the prospect of being liberated from the God
or religion.[3]

A fearful person might ask if it isn't a terrible blasphemy
to speak in this way about religion. Couldn't it mean entering
the path of sin?[4] Lucretius replies that this fear is unfounded.
We may follow our reason without fear. Moreover, religion
itself has been the cause of misdeeds and ungodly acts.[5] We
need only think of Iphigenia of Aulis. On her wedding day,
instead of being brought home in love, she was taken to be
sacrificed at the hand of her own father so that the fleet
might return victorious. Just imagine the crimes which were
brought about by religion rooted in fear and anxiety before
God.[6] The poet says that if one wanted to count up the
whole series of greater and lesser atrocities committed in the
name of religion, the list would go on forever. There is only
one way to free man from the fear of God and to enable him
to live a life of peace and reason, and that is to raise one's
head to Heaven in the knowledge that no power of God can
ever suspend the natural laws. Religion must not be allowed
to limit our freedom.

This means doing away with the burden of the fear of the
gods. For that horrible grimace which stares down insolently
from Heaven and threatens to crush men does not exist. We

may raise our mortal eyes boldly toward Heaven and trample religion under our feet. By that victory we shall be raised to Heaven itself.[7]

The first step toward freedom is the realization that everything which happens on our earth, everything without exception, has a natural cause which can, in principle, be recognized. Nothing which we encounter exists without an operating cause, nothing can proceed out of non-being, nothing comes about as "divine event."[8] The religious man certainly won't subscribe to this; on the contrary, he will see divine process wherever he is incapable of finding a natural explanation. The uncharted areas of his life and his powerlessness to meet the forces of nature with any real effectiveness prompt him to take shelter in religion and prayer. He puts the dwelling place of God in Heaven. He imagines God there, projecting His will into the world, and he believes that in the temple of the gods he experiences divine reality.[9]

But what kind of guarantee are we given by prayer? At the approach of a storm at sea one man begins to string out prayer after prayer, to make vows and promises. Yet he is saved or thrown into the deep by the whirling tempest; he is drowned in exactly the same way as the man who does none of these things. Altars are sprinkled with the blood of animals, temples are built, laws observed. However, all of this comes to nothing. It is useless. How and why should a God be involved with storms, thunder and lightening? Here is proof enough in itself: lightning is just as likely to strike the holy temple as it is the ocean or the mountain peak.[10] God shatters images of Himself as though they were kitchen crockery,[11] despite their being executed with beauty and considerable sacrifice. It would be quite senseless for a God to act this way. No, this is much more compelling evidence of natural causation. The religious aspect of this natural phenomenon, and of earthquakes too, must be done away with. Divine events are not taking place here. The same is true of the year and its seasons, of spring and fall, of day and night, of heat and cold, of fire and water, of air and sea, of the living and the fixed. None of these things are divinely engendered. The final cause of the world's existence goes back to its original components, the atoms, which consist of two principles, the solid and the empty, being and non-being.[12] The same can be said of the heavens and their movements; they arise from the same principles, and God has no part in them as an operating presence.[13]

None of the movement we observe has an eternal duration, not even the earth and the heavens. For just as they came into being, so will they disappear. The day will come when the whole world will be summoned to its death, and the machinery of the universe will crumble.[14] Certainly this will not happen in such a way that nothing is left over. Rather, just as nothing can proceed out of non-being, that which is, is not destroyed. It will go on to make up the creation of the new world-structure. These last particles, the material which constitutes the world, have neither beginning nor end. Rather, all the combinations of it are born, unfold and die.[15]

2 The Failure of Hope

As for this perpetual motion, this disappearance without pause or boundary, cannot the omnipotence of a divine Being bring it to a stop and accord some degree of permanence to man? No, Lucretius answers. Everything has a fixed limit, all power has its end, and the world, closed in upon itself, doesn't admit interference from without.

But is there not something in man which transcends a world closed in this way? In the last analysis, isn't the human soul immortal, and by means of it doesn't man succeed in giving an eternal meaning to his life? Here the answer is, again, No. Man in his body-soul dimension is unquestionably mortal. For the soul is so inextricably bound to the body that the death of one spells the death of the other. Our whole life is imprisoned within corporeality and disintegrates when the body dies. Even if the body is considered essentially different from the soul, nevertheless both of them manifest symptoms of death. Finally, both are bound up in and share this final event. If this were not so, then the soul in dying wouldn't lament its decomposition. No, it would leave the body with pleasure just as a snake sheds its skin.[16] But nothing of the kind happens. Just as the two are inextricably bound in life, so are they bound in death. For life isn't given to any creature as a possession, a thing he may have at his disposal. Life is bestowed on all living entities merely as a gift, a loan for a short time. A period of rigidly fixed duration is assigned us for the use of our life. But then we must bid it farewell and take leave of everything.[17] Our homeland is no longer granted us, nor the house where we are safe. Our sons no longer hurry to us and gladden our hearts, nor do our dead look to us with honor and respect. Nor do we feel the kiss of our dear wives on our lips.[18]

Someone may ask whether this isn't a comfortless picture since we have to leave everything which is close and dear to us. No, Lucretius answers, because the longing for all these things is extinguished in our hearts, as is the desire itself to possess. All our tears have been wept, and the pain which caused us to cry out in despair is gone. All the bitterness of our life is over, all the sadness and dejection, all the misery which we experienced. The last day takes all the suffering from our hearts. Death itself does not reach out and take us, for the soul has proven itself mortal by nature.[19] So we need have no fear or anxiety regarding death. Both the body and the soul lie in the eternal peace of death. A God can no longer reach us, nor are we troubled by uncertainties, nor by the fear of punishment, nor are we anxious about facing a judging God. The end of religious fear is also the end of the fear of death. A new and different *I* will not rise again to its feet. No, as a guest of life we will take leave of our present selves, in equanimity and calm. We shall all, without exception, be followed by other men. No one stays behind, neither the great statesman, the eminent genius who outshone all other men as the sun outshines the stars, nor the begger of the lowest caste—everyone, everyone is mortal.[20]

However, Lucretius explains, if these thoughts don't help you to accept death quietly, then consider what havoc the fear of death plays in your life. You can't bear yourself anymore. Men are always on the run in quest of the new, seizing it, forever in pursuit of life's every charm and pleasure. The thirst for life tortures them, makes them greedy and mean. In their fear of death, men will never have enough of life; they are never satisfied; they always want more; yet, they can't get to the bottom of this quest for possession and become immortal. However, if we realize that our lives are not something we possess, then we can look into the future calmly, without fear. For everything will be summoned to its death.

Though we may reason closely, a long life is no better than a
short one. For if a long life may enable us to obtain more of
what we want, our longings and desires are no more gratified
during it than they are in a life clipped in full flower. All this
can help us to stop running away from this *self*, since we can
never really escape from it.[21] In the calm which we achieve
through contemplation of our nature, God and religion can
bring us no further trouble. Moreover, we are immune to
these powers after our death.

But when everything is over after death and the promise is
not fulfilled by a loving God, isn't there still something left
on this earth whose time won't run out, which isn't doomed
to dissolution?

Isn't it love, somehow, which gives ultimate meaning to
our existence? Step by step, Lucretius proceeds to show us the
hopelessness of love. What happens when two lovers are far
apart? Worry for the beloved creeps into the heart of the
lover. Increasingly the image of the beloved is felt as pain, for
her absence causes life to weigh on the lover as unfulfillment,
and fire eats deeper and deeper into the human heart. He
lives on unhappily, incapable of tending properly to his work,
finding everything burdensome, longing more and more for
her in heart and body. Such a man is deathly sick, and his
cure is out of the question.[22] His love has brought the deepest
suffering into his life.

How do the lovers fare when they are together and their
longing is satisfied? Many men delude themselves here and
imagine themselves happy. But what does this nearness actually bring about? The lovers impart merits to each other
which they don't really possess. An ugly woman can become
beautiful in the eyes of her lover, and a person without honor

can be valued as honorable. But this isn't all. The hopelessness of their behavior expresses itself when they give themselves over to each other, yes, here in the deepest expression
of their love. They can't merge so completely that the one is
immersed in the other, contained in the other, and yet remains himself. The one can't completely gather anything of
the other to himself, can't incorporate anything of the other
in a total way. All striving brings on only distress, exhaustion,
and it ends up leaving man sad and unsatisfied. The wound
inflicted by love is not healed. Once having given himself
over to love, man is caught in a net in which he gets ever
more deeply entangled. Extricating himself becomes impossible, and the more he possesses his beloved, the hotter burn
love's flames.[23] All the joys which the lovers share cannot blind
them to the failure of their final aim. Therefore, it is better
not to yield to one's true love; it is better to turn her away.

This longing is no better satisfied through the love of one's
children. Barren women are wont to seek refuge in religion.
They sacrifice at the altar, burn incense, bring gifts, and pray
to the gods.[24] But this is of no avail, for their barrenness lies
within their own bodies. They, like the lovers, face the lack
of fulfillment of their lives. The love of one's beloved is not a
source of lasting happiness. Moreover, one's inner freedom is
bound up in another, and that person, in turn, is living in a
state of dependency upon us.[25]

Despite this point of view, Lucretius begins his entire
work with a hymn addressed to the goddesses of love, begging
them to help him with his poetry. For love animates everything, and all living things stretch forth their hands toward it.
It causes the sun to shine. The sweet smell of flowers, the
flight of birds, the bright laughter of the sea's surface, the

blowing of the winds—all aspire toward it. Love is the object of all desire and longing, and captivates everything with
its charm. Love, soft and intoxicating, is poured into every
heart. It directs nature in her entirety, and is the source of
everything which has come into existence. The world prospers
through love and love alone, and men are filled with quiet
peace.[26]

Although Lucretius gives us a very tender picture of love,
his work, taken as a whole, offers a three-fold No to the question, "Do our lives have meaning?"

1. God, if he can be assumed to exist at all, has nothing to
do with man. For everything has its natural cause, and its
existence bears no relevance to our own, no connection whatever. For this reason, all religions and religious practices are
deceptions and instil only terror, fear, anxiety and unhappiness
in man. The gods stand mute as to the meaning of our lives.
At the same time, however, this silence represents freedom for
us, since we are alone on this earth.

2. The *Beyond* has nothing to say about the question,
"Why are we alive?" For all hope and, indeed, all sorrows end
with death. Absinthe mixed with honey is, as the poets say,
the answer to the question.

3. In our life here on earth there is no reality which offers
us the possibility of coming to terms with our lives. Love, the
source of everything, is unable to bring us this fulfillment.
Man hasn't the power to give meaning to existence. Only
knowledge of the fragility of everything, only an equanimity
which accepts the wound, only an acceptance that everything
falls into decay—only these can afford us peace and quiet.
One should accept and endure the fact that our existence is
open to question, is not secure, remains unfulfilled.

This, then, is one of the earliest presentations of the atheist's point of view. Two thousand years have elapsed since Lucretius' time. How does the modern atheist see the problem of human living?

3 The Failure of the God-Idea

The most recent, complete system of atheistic thought to be elaborated with an inner dynamism of its own is to be found in the work of the contemporary French poet and philosopher Jean-Paul Sartre. Let us ask him about the meaning of life and see whether he can give us an answer which will settle the question once and for all.

While Lucretius maintained an attitude of cool sobriety in banishing God from the human scene, Sartre's thought is marked by a strong passion, a passion which is Christian in character, but which tries to do away with this tendency within itself. This passion seeks a confrontation with God, but backs away during the quest. It is a passion which longs for a loving God, but which kills love in its own heart.

In his works Sartre brings out all the shock and horror which a man experiences in discovering that God doesn't exist. This experience is like a wound which will never heal. Can a man be said to welcome such a discovery? "No, on the contrary, the existentialist finds it very distressing that God doesn't exist, for with His disappearance goes all possibility of finding . . . values. Nothing good can exist any more (a priori), for the unending and complete consciousness to think it is lacking."[27] Man's awakened consciousness deprives him of the safety to be found in a superior, protecting power. The dream world comes to an end and man understands himself as *Existence*, exposed to danger, naked, thrown into his own resources and extremely lonely. Sartre's student and lifelong partner Simone de Beauvoir describes the terrible discovery which she made at the age of fifteen. "No, it wasn't a fairy tale . . . God became an abstract concept somewhere up in Heaven. One day I did away with Him . . . I have never missed God. He stole the world from me. But one day I realized that in renouncing Him I had condemned myself to death. I was fifteen years old, alone in the apartment, and I gave a cry. When I came to my senses again, I asked myself, 'How do the others manage? How will I come to terms with myself? Am I going to live with this anxiety?' "[28] How *do* the others manage?—this is the question facing the man whose child's world has collapsed and who has discovered that Heaven is empty. And so he casts about for a Being which will draw him back into its protective arms, enabling him to find his life's meaning.

Does *nature* offer us an answer to this question? Can she bring us closer to God and settle this question of the meaning of our lives? In the play *Les Mouches—The Flies*, Zeus conducts Orestes through the world and shows him all the splendors of creation. "Orestes, I created you, and I created all things. Now see! See those planets wheeling on their appointed ways, never swerving, never clashing. It was I who ordained their courses, according to the law of Justice . . . It is my work that living things increase and multiply . . . It is my work that the tides with their innumerable tongues creep

up to lap the sand and draw back at the appointed hour . . .
I make the plants grow, and my breath fans round the earth
the yellow clouds of pollen . . . the world is good; I made it
according to my will, and I am Goodness."[29] The man who
has, nevertheless, become aware of his freedom, who must
make up his mind, cannot find in all this a protecting power
sustaining him. He cannot return to nature and acknowledge
its creator as his king: "You are the king of gods, Zeus, the
king of stones and stars, king of the waves of the sea. But you
are not the king of man."[30] And even if man were created by
the hand of God, his very freedom shows him that he exists,
that he has no further connection with God, and that God
does not provide an answer to his problem. And Orestes looks
God in the face and says, "No sooner had you created me
than I ceased to be Yours."

"I am doomed to have no other law but mine. Nor shall I
come back to Nature, the Nature you found good; in it are a
thousand paths all leading up to you—but I must blaze my
own trail. For I am a man, and every man must find his own
way . . . What have I to do with you, or you with me? We
shall glide past each other like ships in a river, without touching. You are God and I am free; each of us is alone, and our
anguish is akin."[31] So there is no path leading from God to
man and from man to God. Zeus' discourse proves to be only
make-believe. Man and God are alike, each standing on his
own two feet, both of which are broken. Even if there were a
God, nothing would be any different. That is our position,
says Sartre. "Not as though we believe God exists, but we
don't think the question is about whether He exists; man
must rediscover himself and persuade himself that nothing
can save him from himself, even if it were a valid proof for

the existence of God."[32] God cannot enter man's being and affect him from within. Indeed, nature herself, while she seems to manifest God, has slipped out of His hands.

No Being, therefore, will ever find a support for itself, a derivation, an assured existence, a *raison d'être*. "The consciousness expresses that—in anthropomorphic terms—when it says that existence is *superfluous* [*de trop*], superfluous for all eternity."[33] Without doubt, man first makes the discovery of his superfluousness when he searches the world in quest of God. It is here that man learns of his freedom, and here, too, that the meaninglessness of his existence makes itself plain. Thus Zeus says to Orestes, "Poor people! Your gift to them will be a sad one; of loneliness and shame. You will tear from their eyes the veils I had laid on them, and they will see their lives as they are, foul and futile, a barren boon."[34] When man first learns of his Existence and asks himself how he should come to terms with life, he no longer finds God a support. And that is the very secret that God keeps from man, his freedom and absurdity. But if man questions the world, the world throws him back upon himself, and all evasion and refuge are emptiness itself. In a compelling manner, Roquetin, the protagonist of the novel *Nausea*, recounts his experience of the meaninglessness and futility of existence. Seen through his eyes, we were "a heap of existents inconvenienced, embarrassed by ourselves, we hadn't the slightest reason for being there, any of us; each existent, embarrassed, vaguely ill at ease, felt superfluous in relation to the others. Superfluous: that was the only connection I could establish between those trees, those gates, those pebbles."[35] "The word Absurdity is now born beneath my pen . . . Absurdity was not an idea in my head, or the sound of a voice, but that long dead snake at my

feet, that wooden snake . . . And without formulating anything clearly, I understood that I had found the key to Existence, the key to my Nausea, to my own life."[36] "In the snake
I experienced the absolute: the absolute or the absurd."[37] "I
knew perfectly well that it was the World, The World in all
its nakedness which was suddenly revealing itself, and I
choked with fury at that huge absurd being."[38]

"The moment was extraordinary. I was there, motionless
and frozen, plunged into a horrible ecstasy. But in the very
heart of that ecstasy something new had just appeared: . . .
the essential thing is contingency. I mean that, by definition,
existence is not necessary. To exist is simply to be there;
what exists appears, lets itself be encountered, but one can
never deduce it. There are people, I believe, who have understood that. Only they have tried to overcome this contingency
by inventing a necessary, caused Being. But no necessary
Being can explain existence; contingency is not an illusion, an
appearance that can be dissipated; it is absolute, and, conse-
quently, perfect gratuitousness. Everything is gratuitous, that
park, this town, and myself."[39]

Thus Sartre's analysis of Nature and Being, in his termi-
nology "being-in-itself," closes with the absurdity of all existence and the absence of God.

Man's consciousness develops in this state which has no
derivation from or relationship to any other thing and which
is thoroughly meaningless, and it harbors a longing within
itself to find its place within God. The consciousness, however, brings forth Nothingness instead of the fulfillment of its
longing. This Nothingness escapes causal origin, and thus, in
a certain sense, contains the basis of its existence within itself.

The consciousness within a Being tries to find orientation for itself there, and while the Nothingness can be founded, the Being nevertheless remains unfounded, "to no purpose" "too much."[40] The Nothingness constantly and necessarily obsesses the Being.[41] It isn't a sheath which can be thrown off, but lies "in the very center of a Being, in the Being's heart, like a worm."[42] Nothingness, which founds the lack in consciousness and creates (in Sartre's words) being-for-itself, cannot be done away with, and a complete synthesis of being-in-itself and being-for-itself is impossible. Man can never achieve it. This union of for-itself and in-itself would have its foundation within itself, would answer all questions, would be God. However, it is a contradiction, for the in-itself is what it is, and the for-itself is not what it is, and is what it isn't. From this can we say that God doesn't exist? "This contradiction which we brought to light only proves that it cannot be achieved."[43] This means, then, that man will never find his place in God, that he can never "become God," and that God, should He exist, has nothing to do with man. Man's longing, obsessed in her innermost Being by the Being whose longing she is, is not evidence of the actual existence of the one who would be the satisfaction of that longing. All hope for satisfaction later on, for one's having a meaningful existence, is fallacious. Our longing and our striving goes into the totally Empty, into Nothingness [vers le vide, vers le rien].[44]

Man, to the extent that he has to be this Nothingness, is free.[45] The basis of man's freedom lies with this Nothingness dwelling in the heart of his Being. Nothingness also brings out freedom's claim to absoluteness, for freedom is the source of value, meaning and objectives. Determinism, in whatever

form we may encounter it, is never able to set limits upon
freedom. To assume God as the boundary of freedom is
merely to flee from it, this freedom which causes man so
much anguish in that it deprives him of a solid groundwork.
Anguish comes to the fore when I consider my original relationship to meaning and value.[46] For meaning and value are
contained within my freedom. Thus the structure of the
claimed values arises through me and through me alone. My
freedom is the only founder of values, and nothing, absolutely
nothing justifies me in making these values mine and not
those. And since I thus represent the groundwork of value and
meaning in the world without being the groundwork of my
own being, I experience dread.

As Sartre puts it, "ethical dread"[47] develops, dread of the
Nothingness, construed by religion as fear of God. This is the
place for religion or for the hatred of God. The Nothingness
prompts man to try to still this dread through religious practices or revolt. Again and again, Sartre brings out characters
in rebellion against God. Orestes maintains that he is free and
that God Himself can't do anything to a free man. And even
if He had the power to beat man into the dust, man is still a
tough fellow, an obstinate creature who can hate God and
absurd existence along with Him. The emergence of the consciousness of one's freedom, says Orestes, means solitude, the
solitude in which the free man stands. He tells God: "I felt at
one with Nature, this Nature of your making. It sang the
praise of the Good—Your Good . . . To lull me into gentle-
ness, the fierce light mellowed and grew tender as a lover's
eyes. And to teach me the forgiveness of offenses, the sky
grew bland as a pardoner's face. Obedient to Your will, my
youth rose up before me and pleaded with me like a girl who

fears her lover will forsake her. That was the last time, the last, I saw my youth. Suddenly, out of the blue, freedom crashed down on me, and swept me off my feet. Nature sprang back, my youth went with the wind, and I knew myself alone, utterly alone in the midst of this well-meaning little universe of Yours. I was like a man who has lost his shadow. And there was nothing left in heaven, no Right or Wrong, nor anyone to give me orders."[48]

Man knows then that he cannot escape dread and contingence even in the realm of freedom. Man alone determines Good and Evil. Religion credits God with the Good that man does, but the Evil it ascribes to the doer. As for evil, "the Lord declines all responsibility, it doesn't concern him at all, the poor fellow. Yes, Lord, You are completely innocent; how can You conceive Nothingness, You who are fullness itself? Your presence is light, and changes all into light; how are You to know the half-light of my heart? . . . hatred and weakness, violence, death, displeasure, all that proceeds from man alone; it is my only empire, and I am alone within it; what happens within me is attributable to me alone. There—there—I take everything on myself, and I shall never utter one complaint."[49]

Sartre's free man won't put up with this religious confinement and tries to do Good on his own. "And no one in the world has ever done only Good?" he asks.

"No one."

"I'll make a wager with you that I shall. It is obviously the best way to live alone. I was a criminal—I will reform and become a saint."[50]

Man's freedom permits him to do either Good or Evil, but neither gives his existence meaning. Neither can answer the question of why he is alive. Neither offers him a means for coming to terms with life. For man is condemned to freedom. Being free means exactly that, condemned to freedom.[51] But man can't make freedom his founding principle either, for freedom is neither "free to exist or not to exist."[52] The fact of being able to choose freedom would presuppose another freedom, and that another, and so on *ad infinitum*. But if freedom is boundless, I haven't the freedom to choose whether to be free or not. Man *is* his freedom.[53] The origin of freedom is its very existence. However much freedom may be the choice of its Being, it still isn't the groundwork of its Being. "Through the Being it [freedom] is given, it shares in the general contingence of Being, and in doing so, shares in what we call the Absurd."[54] Freedom can exist only as long as it is maintained by contingent Being. Freedom constantly tries to design itself in the direction of Being, which founds it as in-and-for-itself. However, this attempt necessarily fails. God never comes into contact with man, and he himself can never become God. Whereas man remains maintained by contingence in establishing the value and meaning of his existence, man's life, whether considered from the point of view of consciousness or his freedom (and from nature as a whole, as well) loses itself entirely in the meaningless. Death is a further confirmation of this. "Death is the recovery of man's Wholeness by the thing-in-itself, the *en soi*."[55] That is, death is the cessation of Nothingness in the Being, and the Being becomes full again in its contingence and its coincidence. Or, "The eternity which man is seeking is not the infinite duration of this vain running after self, which I myself am responsible for. It is rest in itself, the atemporality of absolute coincidence with self."[56] This spells resolution for the being-for-itself, the *pour soi*. It means that all longing has an end, and everything personal vanishes. At the instant of one's death, the jig is up,[57] *"les jeux sont faits"*! Nothing further will ever happen to us.

We recall Lucretius who had a similar view of death, even if he expected to gain something positive from it. Sartre, on the other hand, cheerlessly maintains that "one always bungles his life when he dies," for "one always dies too early or too late."[58] Our death is always "something tossed into the bargain."[59]

So wouldn't it be better to put a stop to one's life right away? Suicide is meaningless, says Sartre, for it causes one's life to sink into the Absurd.[60] It is absurd "that we are born, and it is absurd that we die."[61] All attempts fail. God never comes into contact with us. Man is left bound up in his solitude and freedom until he returns to the meaninglessness of all Being, and there he must acknowledge he is "superfluous," "useless forever." "I too was superfluous . . . I dreamed vaguely of killing myself, to destroy at least one of these superfluous existences. But my death itself would have been superfluous. Superfluous, my corpse, my blood on these pebbles . . . and the decomposed flesh would have been superfluous in the earth which would have received it, and my bones, finally, cleaned, stripped, neat and clean as teeth, would also have been superfluous; I was superfluous for all time."[62] Nothing is promised man after death, neither by God nor by the Beyond. Is there nothing left for him at all? Or can he expect something in this world, something here and now through contact with a human You? Does love hold out a promise? Since all the channels to God are barred, the channel to another person is all the more open, that is, through loving a You, one finds an ultimate meaning and, in doing so, finds God.

4 The Failure of Love

In the course of our lives we come into contact with other people. The essential thing distinguishing a man from an object is man's ability to look at another person. The Other looks at me. I am reached by the Other not as I would be by an object—on the surface—but in my *Being*.

Through the look or "regard" I know it is You, that the Other is "*what I am not.*"[63]

It may be that I feel myself safe in the look of the Other, or that I am ashamed in front of him, but in any case I experience a Me which is *not* myself, but rather a "Being foreign to my own." I am not the Other, and the Other is not I. And, moreover, when I realize that the Other's Being is contained within mine,[64] I also discover that a void, or Nothingness, stands between You and me, a Nothingness holding us apart. If this Nothingness could be bridged, then in our relationship human Existence would be fully endowed with meaning, and God's Existence would break forth in light within man's. But what really happens? I begin to exist in a world whose center is occupied by the Other. My Being flows off in his direction. He absorbs my Being from me. My Existence, to the degree that it is involved in this contact, finds itself based on a new foundation which lies outside of myself. If I am able to objectify the Other through my look and to incorporate him into my Being, the Nothingness which separates us hampers my recapturing the foundation of my Being. Therefore, the foundation of my Being lies once again "outside" myself, whereas the desire to be my own foundation still lies within me.[65] The "not-you" precludes any real unification. The gap between You and Me, respectively Object-Subject and Subject-

Object, keeps the two parties separate and, at the same time, holds them to making endless attempts to bridge the gap. Thus, a radical separation from the foreign Existence is impossible, as is a final unification.

But in a fragmented contact of this kind, could we not forsee a pure Subject which would not permit itself to be objectified? Sartre says that a Subject which opposes objectification would have to be infinite. It would be God.[66] But what would happen if it were endowed with Existence? Faced with a Subject which would never admit to its objectification, I would become totally Object, for "God's position is accompanied by the hypostatization of my objectivity."[67]

This Subject would constantly look at me as the "eye" of God, and I would have to cringe before it in shame, for certainly my look could never rise to meet its own. I would exist, rendered a stranger to myself, and my Being would "bleed off" into the infinite. The fear of God is founded in this feeling of being totally helpless. Once this God is established, all attempts to escape Him must necessarily fail. But, indeed, this God doesn't exist. There is nobody looking down at man from Heaven. "I supplicated, I demanded a sign. I sent messages to Heaven, no reply. Heaven ignored my very name. I demanded, minute by minute, what I could be in the eyes of God. Now I know the answer: nothing. God does not see me. God does not hear me, God does not know me. You see this emptiness over our heads? That is God. You see this breach in the walls. It is God. You see that hole in the ground. That is God again. The silence is God. The absence is God. God is the loneliness in man. There was no one but myself; only myself . . . if God exists, man is nothing; if man exists . . ."[68]

And man *does* exist. And thus Sartre's play *Lucifer and the Lord* closes with God's death. Man is alone.

Goetz and Hilda, the hero and heroine of this play, want to love each other and, through doing so, overcome their solitude and separation. Goetz, however, protests: "Sleep with you under the eye of God? No; I don't care for drunken couplings. If I could know a night deep enough to hide us from His regard . . ." Hilda replies, "Love is that deep night; when people love each other, they become invisible to God."[69] According to Sartre, in love there is a third disturbing Existence, Do we "become God," in a sense, through our relationship to one another? Are we given a founding principle for our Existence through this union in love? Is God a real presence in love itself, without being a third party? At least then, for as long as love lasts, the question of why we are alive would have an answer, and man, through an Existence he knows to be rightful and meaningful, could come to terms with his life.

How does Sartre see love in operation? We recall how our relationship to people differs from our relationship to animals, stones and trees. As to nature, I confront it as its Subject since it hasn't the power to objectify me. Another man, on the other hand, is Subject and does have this power. Where does he get it? Through *freedom*, which distinguishes him from unconscious nature, from the-thing-in-itself, *l'être-en-soi*. The freedom of the Other can objectify me, seize me through its look and have me become thing-in-itself, *en soi*. The Other has the meaning of my Being in his hands. This meaning, to the extent that it is Existence in the awareness of the Other, remains inaccessible to me. Now if I were able to reach the Subject, You (reach the Other as Freedom without destroying his Freedom), in such a way that he would completely affirm me in his Being and give himself to me, then the Other's Freedom would become the foundation of my Being. The groundwork of my Existence would become present within me, that is, that which is called God would come about within the love-event.[70]

Thus the love-event is based on my recovering my contingence as it was originally established by the Other. Separated from the Other by this "Nothingness" and also interiorly divided by it myself, love grows between the Other and myself. With it develops the love-ideal to destroy this Nothingness, to become fully united without losing one's individuality. But this will always remain an ideal, for our contingence is unconquerable. The love for a contingent creature necessarily contains the seeds of its own defeat.

Nonetheless, Sartre sees a gleam of possibility in love, a possible way to give meaning to our existence. Love seems like a tired but happy smile which—as we see in *Les jeux sont faits*—comes after the lovers have said good-bye for the last time. Nevertheless, all men alike long for this "smile." The lover is not at all content with the mere physical possession of his beloved; he wants her "heart," her freedom. Love is not interested in taking possession of the Other's body. It seeks the complete opening of the Other's person through all the tokens of giving and exchange. But a complete subjugation of the beloved, a servile, selfless passion, would kill the lover's devotion. Tristan and Isolde, chained to one another by the love potion, signify love's destruction. Similarly, it is a blow to love if the lover has to hear "I love you because I voluntarily make it my duty to do so." No, the lover wants the Other to have been determined in freedom to become love. If it happens this way, the You establishes me as absolute reality, the wellspring of all values.

This means that the Other justifies me in my Existence and that in my Being I cease to be "superfluous," cease to be "too much," I am no longer "useless." No, through You I become absolutely necessary to the Other. Thus the Other's Existence imparts itself to me and I lose myself in You who, in freedom, have founded me. Henceforth love fills us with joy.

If this really caused the Nothing within us to come to an end, to be conquered, then in our relationship God would be reality. But our separation will last through all eternity. Thus, love's initial joys turn into perpetual frustrations, for its unattainable ideal is to look directly and lovingly into the Other. I go on, my Existence unjustified. This marks the end of the joy I felt in my complete openness with You, the total giving over of myself to you in serenity and assurance. It is the *fall of man.* Man realizes he is naked. He covers himself so that he may no longer be seen. He hides his real Existence. The You seems to him a risky business. At any moment the look of a third party can suck up the lovers and bleed their Beings dry. Love is doomed to failure for all eternity. In the play *Les jeux sont faits* the lovers are allowed to begin a new life, a "full human life," if they can fulfill one condition, namely, "if they can succeed in loving in complete trust and with all their strength."[73] At first it appears that they might succeed after their trip back to earth, but they fail in the end and return to an altogether meaningless afterlife. Thus you, the Other, become my sorrow instead of my happiness, emptiness instead of the fulfillment of Existence, meaninglessness instead of the meaning of life, a most emphatic *no* instead of a constructive answer to the question of why I am alive, my fall from grace

instead of my justification, "Hell" instead of "Heaven"! "The
fall from grace is the Existence of others," says Sartre. And
the play *No Exit* ends with, "Hell is other people!" Can man
escape this Hell? Might he, if he looked at love in another
way?

We find another approach to this question in Sartre's play
Le diable et le bon Dieu—The Devil and the Good Lord. It
does away with the view that God comes into Being in my
love relationship with you, and stresses the contingent and
the broken in man man's mode of existence. At first Goetz
believes he can reach God through misanthropy and evil.
Then he tries Good. Finally he denounces both ways as absurd. "Love is impossible. Justice is impossible. Try to love
your neighbor, then come and tell me how you made out."[74]
In the beginning, Goetz wants to bring this impossibility
about, for he says, "Goodness is love."[75] He wants this absolute Goodness at any cost. But Hilda, who is love in human
form, advises him that, "one can only love on earth and only
in opposition to God,"[76] that is, in opposition to every claim
to absoluteness, resisting the attempt to flee meaninglessness.
Then and only then can love illuminate man's Existence. He
must exchange God's forgiveness for man's, God's love for
man's—of flesh and blood.[77]

Finally, this new form of love means renouncing Heaven,
not simply in its meaning in the here and now but in the
afterlife too. "I don't want your Heaven . . . I have only scorn
for Your elect—idiots, who have the heart to rejoice when
there are damned souls writhing in hell and poor souls suffering on earth. I belong to the human race, and I will never

desert my fellow beings."[78] Hilda wants to be totally allied
with man and becomes the personification of the love of
one's neighbor, excluding God. Goetz finds love in Hilda,
who says to him, "You have never felt pain . . . but I hardly
feel my own body, I don't know where my life begins or
where it ends . . . but I suffer with all their bodies, I am struck
on all their cheeks, I die with all their deaths. Every woman
you have taken by force, you have violated in my flesh."[79]
And Goetz cries out, "At last, the first one to love me." But
still he doesn't want to pronounce the simple yes of contingent love, and so he complains, "I cannot understand why
we are still two people. I should like to become you, and still
remain myself."[80] Goetz knows this can never be achieved,
that such union is a delusion. So he refuses the love offered
him. He renounces love completely, for it cannot sustain or
heal Existence. "Go," he tells her. "Seek your life and misery
elsewhere." Unshaken in her love, she replies, "For me, you
are the most miserable creature of all. This is my place. This
is where I shall stay."[81]

Goetz wards off this love, despite the hope and joy it offers man, because he is in search of the Absolute. He even
starts to torture Hilda, but he can't get away from her, for
she tells him again and again that she really does love him.
"You realize, don't you," says Goetz, "that I'm taking special
pains to drag you through the dust?" Hilda replies, "Yes,
because I am your treasure." And he knows that as long as
love is at his side, he is not completely lost. Angrily he asks
her, "If I took you in my arms, would you push me away?"
"No." "Even if I come to you with a heart full of impunity?"
"If you dare touch me, that means your heart is pure."

Slowly Goetz comes to understand that love has meaning

only if the desire to attain absoluteness is quenched. And so
he kills God, the presence over him and *within* him. But this
death of the Ultimate only forces him into a still deeper solitude. "If God doesn't exist, why am I alone, I who want to
be with everyone?" And he shouts, "I killed God because He
separated me from other men, and now I see that His death
has isolated me more than I have ever been before. I shall not
allow this huge carcass to poison my human friendship." But
pure human love answers him, "*I* shall be with you." Isolated,
the two of them, their safety unassured, he replies, "You are
myself. We shall be alone together."[82] With full awareness of
the fragility and the contingency of love, but at the same time
giving it her total affirmation, the play closes with this pro-
fession: "I have nursed you, washed you, known the odors of
your fever. Have I ever ceased to love you? Every day you grow
a little like the corpse you will become, and I still love you
with all my heart. If you die, I will lie down beside you, and
stay there to the very end, without eating or drinking; you
will rot away in my embrace, and I will love your carrion
flesh; for you do not love at all, if you do not love the all."[83]

Would one's notion of love change if God were to become
man? Wouldn't that mean that the Nothingness is sustained
by a reality answering all questions? This is the last problem
Sartre raises, dealing with it specifically in his unpublished
play *Barjona.* Yes, if God became man, the thrust would
come from the opposite direction. It would originate in an
absolute You who would gather me up and sustain me in love.
Ultimate reality would become manifest within man, and human love would be God's love. God would take all of man's
suffering on His shoulders. Blood ties would be established.
However we might try, nothing we could do would suffice to

express our gratitude. But still, as we look into the world, what do we see confronting us? Death, yes, death. The world is a weary fall. Man comes onto the scene at a certain point within the fall. No sooner has he appeared than the general fall takes him along with it. He plunges, breaks up and decays.

True, if God were man, there would still be hope, and life would begin again on the far side of despair.[84] Then hope would be man's duty. Christ, the God who became man, would show us the way, for He alone could give meaning to our suffering, He alone could answer the question of why we are alive. Because He would be God and Man, He could do this. As God, He would stand beyond suffering, and we men could overcome pain and meaninglessness to the extent that we are like Him. Our freedom would more than compensate the suffering we felt in the face of the infinite. In this way we could even "do the infinite in." A light would appear for everything made of the flesh. The world would have meaning, and freedom would become love. And if some bitterness remained, if man still felt lonely and abandoned, we could still proclaim the glad tidings that Christ is with us in our suffering. Hasn't He taken all dishonor upon Himself? Our very death would be radiant with joy. Everything, everything would have meaning, and the questioning mind would find its answer in God-man, the divine love.

All of this might have had a certain validity for Sartre back in 1941 when he was in a concentration camp and wrote *Barjona*. But today he strongly repudiates this point of view. We find no support for it, he says, when we look at the life around us. Why do children go on dying of hunger? Why all this wretchedness and injustice? No, he says, it's an absurd position, more absurd than the sum total of man's meaninglessness.[85] The whole world is down on the ground in pain, and nothing has changed since God became man.

> *Earth has its odors . . .*
> *The sun complained to the Lord!*
> *Oh, Lord, let me put out my light,*
> *I have suffered this putrefaction enough.*
> *The more I warm it with my rays, the higher*
>   *its stink rises . . .*
> *The stink of the earth sullies my golden rays.*
> *Woe, woe, cries the sun. My fair circlet*
> *of sunlight has been dragged in the mire.*[86]

Yes, if God were the Ultimate, the Absolute, he would certainly have the power to bring this monstrous Passion play to an end. And Goetz, whom we have gotten to know and who represents humanity, rebels against Him once again, God, the Absolute.

"Useless, yes, men are useless. But what do I care for men? God hears me, and He is the only enemy worthy of my talents. There is only one God and myself! . . . It is God I shall crucify this night, in myself and in twenty thousand men, because his suffering is infinite, and it renders infinite those whom he causes to suffer . . . God knows that, and at this moment He is afraid, I can feel it; I feel His eyes on my hands, His breath on my hair, the tears of His angels."[87]

God is made responsible for all misery. It is He who must ask man for forgiveness, and not the other way around. Yes, even if He had died for mankind Himself, it would have been in vain. A thousand years in Paradise wouldn't wipe out the memory of the suffering on earth. "Did you die for man? Yes or no? Look, men are suffering! You have to die for them again!"[88] However, God doesn't reply. He is experienced as Nothingness, for His becoming man *in the past* has no effect on the world *today*, nor will it give the present man freedom for tomorrow, nor does it offer him hope. "The night, that is what you are, the tormenting absence of all! . . . Huge night of before creation, night of non-knowing, night of disgrace and disaster, devour my foul body . . . for man is made to destroy man in himself, and to open himself like a female to the huge dark body of the night!"[89] "I am going to destroy man, since you have created him to be destroyed."[90]

While man understands God to be this Nothingness, he always breaks when it comes to the God-idea and, worse still, to the idea of God's becoming man. However, God neither exists over us nor has he ever lived as man. "God doesn't exist! This emptiness is God, this silence is God, this absence is God . . ."[91]

Beginning with inanimate nature and continuing on through consciousness, freedom and love until one reaches God who becomes man, everything bears witness to the fact that nothing can save man from himself—no word is spoken, no reply made, no contact offered, for "God is dead."[92] Thus every man becomes a Passion, every man's history a history of suffering. For in trying to escape the question of why he is alive, in trying to reach God, the Absolute, man designs himself in such a way that he will go to ruin. In this way, man's Passion is quite different from Christ's, for man wants to lose his human-ness, so that God might be born. But his powers are never strong enough to throw off Existence in all its absurdity to reach God and equal Him. There is no good reason why man is given this longing, no reason for his Passion, no reason for the freedom and love which stems from his longing. Man is a *useless longing*, a meaningless emotion. *"L'homme est une passion inutile."*[93]

There is no God above him. He has nothing but the earth. True, earth does offer him the possibility of love, but still only in that form which makes no claim to absoluteness, a love, therefore, which is merely human—contingent and meaningless in accordance with man's own cycle of appearance, blossoming and withering up. It can give man only a glimmer of light which God will ignore throughout eternity.

5   The Fulfillment: Yahweh Is God

Probably all of us, in the course of our lives, have felt something of the abandonment of which we have spoken, this silence from God. No doubt, we have all been weighted down at different times by the question which Lucretius formulated at the time of Paul the Apostle, and we have suffered life's apparent meaninglessness as it is expressed in our time by Sartre. In our hearts we have been downcast and bitter. Is there really no answer? Is our cry swallowed up by the void? Does only our echo return?

With Lucretius the question of the meaning of life is centered around religion and the picture of God arising from it. Sartre's revolt, the bafflement of a perpetually "incomplete" life, is aimed directly at God and at God's becoming

man. Both questions speak to our situation which seems to
be threatened by the loss of religion, by secularization and by
atheism. Is there a living faith today whose practice offers us
an answer? Is there a word which gives us hope and brings us
face to face with a God who is love? Is there a word abroad
today which doesn't do away with the unknown god but
which proclaims him in the glad tidings of love, because
God's word is manifest in our lives? Is the net of religion
really sound, or does it threaten to tear there where Christ
stands on the shore?

Certainly attempts to define the meaning of religion differ widely. If one takes it as an openness to contact with God,
expressed in man's action, then it means a deep faith, iden-
tical to religion and understood as a gift. But in Lucretius
and in others today we have another concept which sets the
basis of religion in the religious experiences, acts and needs
of man, encouraging him to try to establish contact with God
on his own initiative. Religion, according to this concept, refers to that power which can raise man out of his despair. To
quote Bonhoeffer, "Man's religiousness orients him toward
God's power within the world."[94] In experiencing his helplessness, impotence and indigence, man encounters a boundary to his existence. Beyond this boundary are expanses of
unending question and doubt which he tries to hold off with
the help of religion. This doubt gives rise to a perception of
God which reflects man's weakness, frailty and incomplete-
ness. God is thought of as a boundary. But man can experience the boundary only in its ambiguity, a strict ambiguity,
for he doesn't know whether this superior power is supposed
to mean love or hate, pardon or judgment. Lucretius describes the horrors carried out in the name of different re-

ligions. None were exempt from this, and these atrocities remind us to be careful about considering religious practices as though there were absolutes. The Old Testament itself speaks of human sacrifice, and history gives us ample evidence both of men persecuted for their religious practices as well as of the misuse of religion as a means to inspire fear and to suppress freedom of conscience. It would be just as one-sided and false to mistake man's religious inclination for such abuses as it would be to deny this inclination or belittle its positive value. But as long as it has the construction just described, as long as religion has its roots in human needs, as long as God must or ought to spring into the gap where human thoughts and powers fail, man will not be given an answer. Acting through his acquisitive nature, man wants to come to terms with the boundary. Therefore, it can be characteristic of a religion to stake out a certain limited area wherein man can proceed to that necessary business of rounding himself out, of turning despair away. His lack of Existence enables him to understand this fullness. His indigence allows him to understand Him who needs nothing, and his weakness has him understand God's strength. For a religious world, circumscribed in such a way, God is the Great Unknown, never coming into contact with man, always beyond the boundary of human powers, worshipped out there merely as an unknown force.

The man of faith criticizes this widely held and practiced concept of religion and the notion of God arising from it. He insists that God is something else, something quite different from the way man, in his religiosity, pictures Him. Theodore Lessing was addressing the sceptical but "religious" man when he wrote:

> You child of fear and woe
> Yourself, you are your creed,
> You fabricate your God
> Then worship at his knee

Scripture, both the Old and New Testament, speak out against this characteristically human religiosity and the concrete forms through which it is expressed. And if the Old Testament is uncritical in many points in describing God's work according to prevalent religious representations of Him, nevertheless the prophets repeatedly express their reservations concerning sacrifice and religious observances, a reservation which places particular concern on single persons, on widows and orphans of false religious practices. Obedience, compassion, and the heart's loving devotion are closer and more pleasing to God than burnt offerings and other religious ceremonies. "Burnt offering and sin offering hast thou not required" (Psalms 40,6). "To what purpose is the multitude of your sacrifices unto me?" (Isaiah 1, 11). "The most High is not pleased with the offerings of the wicked; neither is he pacified for sin by the multitude of his sacrifices" (Ecclesiastes 34, 19). "To obey is better than to sacrifice" (1 Samuel 15, 22). And, finally, the word of prophet Hosea (6, 6) brings forth the final truth which deprives religion of its claim to absoluteness: "It is love that I desire and not sacrifice." Jesus holds this word up to the Pharisees to show them God's love and compassion for sinners from birth onward. The rigid, legal character that religion may secretly have is brought into the open in the revelation wherein God opens Himself and appears before man. Man's attempt to answer the final questions is shown for what it really is—a deception.

Thus it is true that Yahweh-God "spells a major crisis for all religions, or, put in a different way, the disclosure of Himself brings the answer to religion along with it. In those parts of the world where religion has never taken hold, we don't find the flaming autumn colors of the atheist's pride. And, conversely, wherever we find pride, either in its demonic or its tranquil form, in aggressive or melancholy trappings, we find ourselves in the presence of a religion. Yahweh bars the way to one as He does the other. But it seems that today, before the human spirit can become earnest with the name of the unknown God, it must first be thrown off the tracks by nihilism."[95] It was this earnestness that Christ desired when he cleaned out the temple and turned over the money-changers' tables. The disputes, and the quarrels over keeping the Sabbath, warn one not to set up religious practice as an absolute nor to consider it an answer to the fundamental question of the meaning of life. The publican's prayer seems to renounce a personal self-initiated attempt at contact with God and to express merely the simple awareness of having been denied love and, therefore, to be a sinner. But how strongly does the Pharisee's prayer differ from this! Even when the Samaritan raised the difficult question about the appropriate place for the worship of God—"Our father worshipped in this mountain; and ye say, that in Jerusalem is the place where men ought to worship" (John 4, 20)—Jesus gives an answer which makes this question relative and requires a worship "in spirit and in truth" (John 4, 23).

From the foregoing we recognize that religious life and forms do, indeed, have their own meaning, but that when God reveals Himself, stepping forth into view, then religion is "synthesized" in the Hegelian sense of the word. Indeed, it

still owes us the answer to why we are alive, for it cannot
ask man to recognize its claim to absoluteness, and yet it
must be the absolute and final answer to our question. At the
same time, hope is given to all who are not "religious," who
have no access to this "special world," hope that they may
make contact with God in another way. On the other hand,
the notion of a God who comes forward to console us in the
difficult moments of our lives, who offers us asylum in our
anguish and despair—in short, a God who inhabits the human boundary and acts on man's behalf when his powers
fail—such a God must remain unknown. He is not a God
of the living, but of the dead.

So Lucretius, with his "religious" notion of God, had to
fail and, with him, all who think of God as a boundary and
see the relationship between God and man in a context of
power versus helplessness. For here God is only question, the
entire openness to question of man's life.

But how does God make Himself known to man? The
more carelessly one banters His name about, the emptier
does the whole God-concept become. The reality it should
symbolize gets worn out and merges into the colorless shadows.
There are good reasons why some people today prefer not to
use the word "God," for it begins to evoke a false god. In
Scripture, particularly the Old Testament, the name "God"
is understood as a proper name, distinguishing it from "godhood" or "deities." Yahweh is the nameless name one never
dares to pronounce. It is the proper name for God whose
presence is known as a certainty by the people, in that they
are the chosen. According to different interpretations, the
content of the name "Elohim," which is closer to the notion

of "godhood," is derived from "Yahweh," the Lord. A predicate is added to "Yahweh," this name one doesn't dare to pronounce—namely the predicate that he is "God." Yahweh is God! But in the Old Testament the subject and the predicate are not turned around. It cannot be said that God is Yahweh. Rather, Yahweh, the Lord, is God. If this identification could go both ways, then the road would stand completely open to the notion of a god who is merely man's projection of himself. This is precisely what Scripture wants to avoid, this misinterpretation of a "religious" idea of God. Indeed, the Lord who is God is the converse of this idea, for He is, at the same time, the most known and the most unknown. Unknown in that His Being escapes description, as it is particular to "gods"; known in that He is present as the Lord of the Chosen and determines their acts and Being.

The story of Moses' calling offers us an example of this. This is the only place in the Old Testament where God's name is explained.[96] During the exchange, Moses asks God about His name, and the answer he receives is not an adjective or a noun, but rather a verb, a verbal form which points toward the future. Let us bring this story to mind: "And Moses said unto God, Behold, when I come unto the children of Israel, and shall say unto them, the God of your fathers hath sent me unto you; and they shall say to me, What shall I say unto them? And God said unto Moses, *I will be there as he who is there:* and he said, This shalt thou say unto the children of Israel, I AM HERE has sent me unto you" (Exodus 3, 14–15). Without doubt, the name, "I AM ——" constitutes a refusal to answer the question. Yahweh will not let Himself be contained by the expression "God" and be arranged within the hierarchy of godly beings. Thus

Gollwitzer aptly says, "Although it [the Biblical mode of speech] invariably speaks of God as a [objective] Being-standing-opposite-one and as a [objective] *Real Being* . . ., its avoidance of an objective speech from God, of a description of the essence of godhood, is a method for preserving the uniqueness of that which it calls God and to guard the relationship to Him—*Deus non est in genere.*"[97] If Moses had taken God's answer primarily as a metaphysical description of His essence, as a predicate which cast God's essence as Being, we would have no idea why Moses acted as he did; we would not know what motivated him to go to the Pharaoh. But also a voluntary misunderstanding, something like "I, Yahweh, am as much as I want to be," would not satisfy the meaning of the predicate. So, does Moses depart without an answer? No, rather he receives an enormous promise, a promise which sets his action into ontological distinction from all purely inner-worldly happenings. His relationship to the people is not the banal relationship between a leader and the masses, but has its own depth, promising freedom and salvation. His going to the Pharaoh is not an event in the standard measurements of the world—no, the Lord, who is God, appears in it. In this relationship God is revealed to Moses. Were he to shrink away from contact with his people, God would sink into the unknown, and Moses' life would have miscarried. But Moses goes, acting in the knowledge that his action will give freedom to his neighbor, the people, and open new possibilities for them. The promise of God's being with one means quite concretely His presence. God will enter in through Moses' act of giving, but through no other way. Certainly this "entering in" in the future, does mean a merging into inner-worldly action, but an entering into the world which is not

God. His Operating-Being enters into the world of man. God opens Himself in the fullness, not the "leanness," of His willingness to be with man, in the fullness, not the leanness, of this relationship. His promise is, "I will be there." To prevent one's construing this to mean that in the future, in this God-man relationship, man could finally take God unto himself, God added, "I will be there as he who is there." He will be there at all times and in all places where salvation is to be granted. This promise means that, in the fullness of human relationships, all boundaries and contingence will be dissolved and man will be allowed to contact the Absolute, the Final, the Eschatological.

Moses' entire life warns us, however, not to take this "synthesis" in an undialectic sense. The limitedness and relativity of all action continued just as before, and Moses was still weighed down by uncertainty. When he acts in his own name and does not rely on the promise, his limitedness and contingence become absolute and he forfeits the promise and, with it, God. But then again, when he answers the situation, when he is focusing on his "being-with-Others" and not on himself, when he gives himself completely to the people, then a final meaning expresses itself within the fragility of his action. Then the absolute Lord, who is God, becomes present. This Lord is not to be had by the acquisitive in man, but steps forward in the situation, giving Himself as a gift.

How different this is from Lucretius' and Sartre's perception of God. Lucretius denies the possibility of contact with Him, and thus excludes himself from a final contact. He showed us that one shouldn't conceive of God as an agent bringing meaning into the difficult moments of one's life. Lucretius is justified in his efforts to destroy religion, justified to the extent that he rejects a god whom men have erected for their own fulfillment, their "own" god, as it were. He considers this only a would-be answer to the question of why we are alive. Sartre's views on the problem of God have a similar ring. God arises out of human longing, out of a deficiency in Being. In God, man seeks a means for giving a grounding principle to his Existence, a foundation, a source for his consciousness, a basis for his freedom and for the fulfillment of human intercourse and love. Sartre can rightly say that this god doesn't exist, that he is only the unstilled longing of the human heart, that when he fails he reveals his true essence—Nothingness. This denial of a god who is man's self-projection has its justification in those cases where one forms a notion of God through one's desire to "have" him, through one's acquisitive nature. God suffers through man's impulse toward self-fulfillment, in being degraded to a "need."

This denial, however, can be the turning point in one's arriving at a genuine notion of God. In Scripture, God appears as an Unknown Being and manifests Himself in the fullness of human acts and human willingness to "be there" for others. When a man is completely "there," when he doesn't flee from his situation but holds out through all joy and despair, God enters in, Yahweh the Lord, and the man understands he is no longer alone and that he is not living without purpose. And although this man is sure that God will be there, just as Moses was sure of it, till he cannot count on God being available for him when he wants Him, for God gives Himself, again and again, as an ever-renewed gift in man's contact with his neighbor. The answer is not found in an objective system which one can employ at will, nor in the abstraction of one's concrete situation, but in the answer to

the situation. It is through meeting the concrete demands
that man receives the Lord, ever *his* Lord and God. While it
is true that his action is backed up by the word of God, man
experiences the word concretely in his contact with others as
the answer to the meaning of his life. If the existential structure of the concrete situation is not realized existentially,
then we have only would-be answers, or a foregoing of any
answer, any deliverance.

6 The Fulfillment: Jesus Christ Is Our Neighbor

But how is this possibility of bringing forth God's presence
open to us today? Of the many answers offered, which one
will sustain my Person, my Being, in the deepest way? What
kind of action is it which will bring forth God's presence?
The answer lies only in another person, never in a configura-
tion of circumstances, a doctrine or a *Weltanschauung*. Only
a You can provide an answer. For the believing Christian, this
You is Jesus Christ. Through Jesus, man escapes a merely
inner-worldly interpretation of human relationships, and a
casting of the Lord—the Lord who is God—into a back-
ground of myth derived from the Docetists. The Old Testament, which sees Yahweh as the one who opens the future,
is looked at in a sharply different light. And when the Lord,
who is God, is present in historic confrontations with man,
the structure of the relationship is nevertheless restricted to a
limited area, and the insight into the contact situation does
not seize it in its fullest possibilities.

The notion of the contact situation can also be found in

mythical form in the religions around Israel. God is contacted
in man. Godhood disguises itself in mortal form. In this
shroud, the unknown God visits the human scene. A man's
damnation or salvation is decided, unbeknownst to him, by
his treatment of this "god-in-one's-neighbor." And if, in this
mythical picture, neither the god's manner of determining a
person's salvation nor the neighbor are taken in complete
seriousness, still the idea is there that the god is contacted in
one's fellow man. But here again the notion is not thought
out thoroughly, for only in certain instances does this situation come about as both a favor to and test of *the few*, while
the everyday fellow man lacks this dimension of "the Divine."

Jesus Christ spelled the lifting of the restrictions in the
Old Testament and in the myths. A man open to other men
is seen as one identifying himself with the Father, with
Yahweh the Lord, with God. The faithful consider that Jesus
and God are one and the same Being. From now on, veritable
blood ties link man and God. Together they constitute a total, lasting unity. God is no longer the unknown out on man's
boundaries, but is present in the heart of life, the center of
life. God becomes man. Nevertheless, man's desire to have
some access to God grows stronger and stronger, this demand
for some way to "see" Him, so that one might convince himself of His presence. This is expressed in Philip's request:
"Lord, show us the Father and it sufficeth us. Jesus said unto
him, Have I been so long time with you, and yet hast thou
not known me, Philip? He that hath seen me hath seen the
Father; and how sayest thou *then,* Show us the Father? Be-
lievest thou not that I am in the Father, and the Father in
me?" (John 14, 8,10). With this assertion, God becomes
man's neighbor, God being present in the man Jesus. At the

same time, this sets God off at an immeasurable distance
from man because, from now on, any direct access to Him
is denied man except through the man Jesus, for only in
Jesus Christ does God manifest Himself turned lovingly
toward us. This testifies to the presence of God, the Lord, and
offers man a new possibility in his quest for the meaning of
life. The union between Jesus, the son of man, and the word
of God gives us a vertical "third dimension" to our horizontal
perception of man and God, sparing us the distortion of a
"two-dimensional map" with uncharted areas.

But if Jesus had not given the believer a second identification, God's permeation into all of human existence would
have sunk into the past, would have degenerated into another
of the mythologies recorded in history. In the Gospel according to St. John, Jesus says that it is good for the Apostles
and for all who believe in Him that He go, good that His
historical form should sink into the past, for He is giving
Himself over to death. The idea of the Kingdom of Israel,
here on earth in its brilliance and power, the immediateness
of the Kingdom of God, came to its end on the cross. "Nevertheless I tell you the truth; it is expedient for you that I go
away" (John 16, 7). It is this very distance between the historical appearance of Jesus and those who believe in Him
which makes possible the indestructible unity between the
man in contact with me and the contact with Jesus. The
conditional, the ephemeral, yes, even the accidental, all afford
us contact with the Final, the Absolute—that is where God enters in, God who becomes man. This is why Jesus must depart, that He might be with us in our weakness and impotence and give us His help.[98] It is not the omnipotence of
God, His wholeness, which grants us salvation, but His im-

potence and feebleness, His suffering. Thus the promise of
salvation should not be taken as the answer to our insuffi-
ciency, our contingency and our suffering. God's power and
glory enter these qualities. Man is not freed from the dialectic, but, in fact, runs into it here, for the One entering the
ephemeral, entering the broken existence of man's life question, is not an unknown god. No, it is He who conveyed
Himself to man as love.

Thus, when Dostoyevsky bids us to "look to suffering for
our happiness," he is expressing a deep insight which is borne
out by our lives. Happiness is found in the transient which we
constantly cling to and which vanishes before our eyes. Happiness is found in all the ephemeral things which blossom up
in our lives and fade away. Here is a dimension which proclaims the Ultimate and gives us the Absolute as a partici-
pating presence. This is what Jesus wants to show us in his
departing. He goes as far as death in his giving of himself, to
be present in the human action of two disciples on the road
to Emmaus. Christ revealed himself in Mary Magdalene's
encounter with the gardener. The story of Christ's resurrection tells of a new meaning in human life, with its key in human relationships. The Gospel tells of it, too, the most dis-
parate sections giving us this picture of the word of God
become flesh. Christ knows Himself ever-present in contact
between people. As the Final in that which is open to question. If we are met by a child, and say yes to him, we gather
the heart of life into ourselves. "And whosoever shall receive
one such little child in my name receiveth me" (Matthew
18, 5). So, too, we receive Christ in our willingness to receive
a disciple of Christ. The person who is open to the word of
the Other receives the word of God. "Verily, verily, I say unto

you, He that receiveth whomsoever I send receiveth me; and
he that receiveth me receiveth him that sent me" (John 13,
20). But a man who doesn't love his neighbor, who would
persecute him, depriving him of his freedom, is also perse-
cuting Him who would give his life its final meaning. "Saul,
Saul, why persecutest thou me?" (Acts 9, 4) He who looks
down on his fellow man and persecutes him is directing his
contempt at the Ultimate Reality. But the person who is receptive to the word of a You, who has been given ears to
hear it, finds God with him. "He that heareth you heareth
me; and he that despiseth you despiseth me; and he that
despiseth me despiseth him that sent me" (Luke 10, 16). It
is quite explicit that at the last judgment our salvation or
damnation will be decided by how we treated our neighbor.
"Then shall the King say unto them on his right hand, Come,
ye blessed of my Father, inherit the kingdom prepared for
you from the foundation of the world: For I was hungry, and
ye gave me meat: I was thirsty, and ye gave me drink: I was a
stranger, and ye took me in: Naked, and ye clothed me: I was
sick, and ye visited me: I was in prison, and ye came unto me.
Then shall the righteous answer him, saying, Lord, when saw
we thee hungry, and fed *thee?* or thirsty, and gave *thee* drink?
When saw we thee a stranger, and took *thee* in? or naked, and
clothed *thee?* Or when saw we thee sick, or in prison, and
came unto thee? And the King shall answer and say unto
them, Verily I say unto you, Inasmuch as ye have done *it*
unto one of the least of these my brethren, ye have done *it*
unto me" (Matthew 25, 34–40). The same words, in a negative sense, are directed at those who failed to cover the
stranger and the naked with love, at those who did not
minister to the sick but extolled their own good deeds and

sacrifices, who did not visit the prisoner, who did not quiet the longing of the hungry, the thirsty and the forsaken. All human action which takes place in a contact situation inevitably means contact with the Ultimate, the Absolute. God is present in such a relationship. A profound message is given us in the Book of Proverbs (19, 17): "He that hath pity upon the poor lendeth unto the Lord."

All these statements express the notion of a God whose presence is with us in the center of our lives. In a service of love we come into contact with Him, with Jesus Christ. Just as it is illegitimate for a sinner to make use of an "as though" for his justification, and thus to reduce the process of justice to a farce, so would it be false and distressing if we were to love our neighbor "as though" he were Christ. No, Christ sees Himself in a deep union with a You receptive to contact. And this is how God is to become Reality for us in the center of our lives, become the Final Depth. But still, this union of a human You and the Reality of God should not be thought of as a state, so that one's neighbor is taken as an independent and unrelated thing, an absolute phenomenon, for the dialectic union of the conditional and the unconditional is brought about *within* man's actions. What ye have done unto the least, ye have done unto me. Contact with God is realized in the love relationship between human beings.

For the contingent man, this contact can certainly have two sides to it. In entering the contact, he can encounter openness or closedness, love or hate, stemming from the You; but real contact with God takes place only in *the action of love.* God cannot be present, even in the inter-human relationship, when a man closes himself to the Other's Person, when he will not permit himself to be relative, that is, will not let himself relate, and such a man is really an a-theist— without God—alone with the question of his life's meaning. The final undialectic answer is absurd Existence; in other words, his answer is despair.

Both attempts to escape this despair fail: flight into direct communion with one's fellow man, and the attempt, despite everything and on one's own initiative, to beat a path straight up to God. These two extremes resemble each other in that they are not open to the word of God, The word which would open up space for a true contact with Him. They are only seeking the "God for me," and they run up against the boundary-concept of the unknown god without reaching the real life which the message of Christ proclaimed. To be sure, a "contact with God *in* one's fellow-man" can be correctly understood and brought about, but the term is inaccurate, since one is in danger of finding God only under the skin of one's fellowman. This would mean that the Other is only "used," or rather, misused, being either a practice ground for one's *self*-realization or constantly bringing untoward effects to bear on the "love of God." Nowhere is this grounded in a clearer, more explicit manner than in God's becoming man. Here God does not use man, merge into human form or destroy him. A man and wife do not merge into each other in the expression of their deepest love, but develop their Person in their mutual entering of the other—and thus does God enter man in love.

The Person is approached as You, and taken in all seriousness, and not misused as a means. One is hedging if he says, "You ought to do it for the Church," "for the Kingdom of God," "for God," and not for the man open to concrete contact. One is being uncharitable to his neighbor, and misuses him, and personally degrades him. Love causes the vertical plane to break into the horizontal, and human relationships partake of a new token of Ultimate Reality. In God's son, in God's becoming man, we have His promise that when love inspires a contact, then He, Yahweh, is present, then the Lord is our neighbor and is with us. Jesus Christ is our neighbor! This sentence, too (like Yahweh is God), cannot be turned around. Its converse is possible only in action, if it has its cause and existence in irreversibility. In the act of love the neighbor proves himself as "more," proves himself "the Lord," proves himself Jesus Christ, because God is there in the contact as a Person. However, if one were to maintain that the Other *is* Jesus Christ, then one would either lapse into a pat religiousness, into the clichés recommended in books of piety, or interpret it as a humanist would, depriving the Christ-event of its proper character. If Christ is taken as a certain kind of openness and sympathy toward one's fellow man, and if that is the last word to be said on the matter, one is embracing atheism, and the depth of human existence is gone. If God is automatically included as a human being in one's communion with one's fellow-man, we are in the presence of a false god, an idol.

We should consider—and not just to guard against God's degradation into a simple inner-worldly communication with one's fellow man, but also to guard against a contact with God which excludes our neighbor—we should consider the fact that the love of God and the love of our neighbor are realized in one and the same act. The concrete claim of a You is heard in love and becomes an absolute event.

If Ludwig Feuerbach maintained that God has no meaning as a subject, only as the predicate of a statement, it was because he wanted to understand God's presence. In saying this, however, he destroyed the structure of the contact as a partly-human, partly-divine thing. He also said that God was his first thought, reason his second, man his third and last. With this, the one precept of the love of God and the love of one's neighbor is cut to pieces and killed. That was the only way he could describe the Divine as a tension between man and mankind. Thus, God becomes an abstraction, a Being out beyond the limits of man's power. He is seen arising out of a lack in man. This is what will befall us if the tension, in which God is an operating presence, is left out between mankind and man. God enters into contact in the situation where a You expresses an absolute claim.

The parable of the Good Samaritan is an effective weapon against attempts to undermine the Christian faith, against attacks on the Final Depth as it has been given to man. That we might reach the true life and find meaning in human action, this is what is asked of us: "Thou shalt love the Lord Thy God with all thy heart, and with all thy soul, and with all thy strength; and thy neighbor as thyself" (Luke 10, 27; compare Deuteronomy 6, 5; Leviticus 19, 18). (And this follows upon it immediately in the Hebrew text: "I am Yahweh," or "I will be there.") To explain this act of love, Jesus speaks of the Samaritan who set out on the road from Jerusalem to Jericho and quite naturally, without thought as to the circumstances, helped a man who had been robbed and beaten by thieves. Through his compassion the Samaritan became the man's neighbor. There on the road from Jerusalem to Jericho, on the road of compassion (traveled by a priest and a Levite on their way from the temple, both of whom passed by on the other side), God was present and they passed Him by; love did not take place, there was no possibility whatever of contact with God. But when two men were gathered there on that road, Christ was with them, deeply with them.

No abstraction or theory has space enough for this quite concrete event, not even if one tries to explain Being, not God, as *the* neighbor (Heidegger). Here one's neighbor is depersonalized and thought of as *the* neighbor, and the claim of a You is neatly and properly muffled up into silence. God keeps silent, too. How clear is Jesus' answer to this as he closes the parable, saying, "Go and do thou likewise." This is all one needs for finding the Unquestionable in all that is open to question, for contacting the Unconditional in the conditional.

So unconditionally is the conditional established within the contact situation that one would forego everything to take one's erring neighbor unto oneself in absolute love and grant him salvation. Moses and Paul both dared to pray in the following manner: "Forgive them their sins; and if not, blot me, I pray thee, out of the book which thou has written" (Exodus 32, 32). "For I could wish that myself were accursed from Christ for my brethren, my kinsmen according to my flesh" (Romans 9, 3). When this willingness is felt, love is present, love abounds. The person is ready to stake the whole of himself, everything, that his brother might come into contact with love once in his life, and with it, come into contact with Final Reality. There is no legal cramping up here, no, nor any of Sartre's kind of cramping which rejects happiness because of suffering, and which revolts. There is nothing of this kind to be found here, only complete devotion for him who needs love, again and again, love. This is not an exaggeration; it is the very same principle which Jesus expressed in saying, "Greater love hath no man than this, that a man lay down his life for his friends" (John 15, 13). And Paul took this to mean the whole breadth of life, even life proper.

Here we have come upon the boundary and the final possibility for experiencing God's presence in the heart of our lives, and we are bidden to do likewise to the neighbor who comes into contact with us.

7 The Fulfillment: God Is Love

If, up to now, there has been some ambiguity in the way we have spoken about God's presence in our lives (in that God is also present in the *rejection* of contact, the rejection of love, which causes the Ultimate to miscarry horribly), then it has become increasingly clear that God is really perceived only where there is love. Only then does He step forward from His concealment, for God is love. That is His name— love. To every man He says, "I have loved you with eternal love. And if your father and your own mother were to forget you, I am with you, and I shall always be with you."

This sentence, "God is love," is another which cannot be turned around. Yahweh is God, and God is present in our contact with our neighbor, for in Jesus Christ he became our neighbor. Touched by God's love, we receive the promise that He is love. If one were to turn the sentence around, one would become a pantheist, and love would evaporate into the universal, the abstract. God's personal Being makes such an inversion impossible. For certainly inherent for us in the act of love is our seeing God, His presence *in* love, as its original source.[99] Man knows that in love he receives fullest affirmation. In living for others he knows "absurd existence" to be meaningful. This *contacting* aspect of human existence is given final depth and clarity in the love relationship and in the affirmation that love, not solitude and despair, is the final word to be said about man's condition—for God is love. Indeed, the word "love" is no less misused than the word "God."

Generosity, beauty, intelligence, character—these qualities are attractive to man. He longs for them and, because he lacks goodness, he craves them and calls his craving "love." Here, again, this is the "love" arising out of deficiency, for solitude speaks from the heart. A man or an object is "loved." Just as a concept of God originating in man's deficiency puts forth an unknown idol, love, too, is empty if we "love" a man for his "lovableness," his willingness to sacrifice everything, his magnanimity or his ability to understand everything. That is not love's innermost soul, but the craving of the human heart, restless and desiring the end of its wishes and dreams. Whenever You are used to confirm myself, to bring me satisfaction, to ease my need and despair, love is struck in the face. Love outlasts all disappointments, the loss of beauty, honor and reputation. Love gives you time and expecting nothing, nevertheless endures. Love remains faithful in sickness and in suffering—this is what love is and this is what God is. Attempts to found or justify love only destroy it. One is not loving with his innermost soul if one loves the other person for qualities that person possesses. Of course, it would be false and abstract to exclude Your beauty and good qualities, but they must never be my final reason for giving the You my acceptance and my support. The only answer to proceed out of fullness, out of the innermost part of life, says, "I love you because You are, because You are this unique irreplaceable person." To love means to say, "It is good that You exist." Yes, it is good. Why? Does the person who loves become richer through it, or does he obtain fulfillment or some sort of advantage? Will he advance more rapidly in his career? No, that isn't why it's good that the other person exists. But why, then? Is it good because the person who loves can be with the other person just as he is, because the other person doesn't want anything from him, because the other lets him be free?

No, in love this isn't the essential thing. The person who loves obtains no *thing* from the other, no "something." Rather, it is he himself whom he receives from that person. Before he began to love, he was, so to speak, not himself. One might say he *was* only the role he had to play for himself and for the world. But as soon as he begins loving, he *is*. He loves. Thus, he is. And the same is true for the other person. This means something inestimably precious: the one receives himself from the other in a two-way giving. Both are in that they constitute a We with each other. Their Being is called "being-with." Love first comes about when two people in accordance with their Being pronounce the word "We." This use of We expresses a final commitment. I want to be "with" you and would like, too, that you be "with" me. From this moment on I belong to you. I am always available to you, and from now on you will never be alone. Even if we are separated by distance, yes, even by death itself, I am always "with" you. Everything that I am and have is here at your disposition. And I know that I shall always remain in you and that I am safer in your hands than I am in my own.

Love, in the pronouncement of this We with its newly acquired Being, brings forth a new space for existence. The entire world receives a dimension of the Deep.[100] God is known
as love. He manifests Himself *in* love *as* love. One's neighbor, loved as he is, unfolds a truth from within his Person, a
truth which outweighs all that is incomplete, finite, contingent and weak. Here an absolute Yes is spoken, eternal, never
to be withdrawn. And where the Ultimate dawns in man's
temporality, God is present. When the light, the light called
love, begins to shine on man's absurd existence, the question
of why we are alive is answered in full. Love, as it has been
described in its deepest form, includes rather than excludes
the Samaritan's love, the act of simple service. Love is present
in the fullest way in those unplanned encounters where one
person performs a service of love for another. The final Yes
is extended out toward man. He is offered the promise that
Yahweh will be with him if man can only hold himself to
His contact, if he can only wait, wait until death if need be,
although perhaps, only until the wakening of his Person's
Being. For one's neighbor is here, initiating contact, receptive
to it, offering one the possibility to "come to terms with life."

Isn't that saying too much? What about the people who
are failing left and right, who, in their despair, seek refuge in
Another, only to find themselves thrown back again onto
their own Persons? What about all the people who are disap-
pointed by life? This can only be answered by a person who
is in the situation and knows the *nevertheless* of love.

Once I met a married woman who had given everything
to her husband and knew her love for him wasn't reciprocated. "Still, all I want is for him to be happy," she said,
"even if I am unhappy myself. I'll continue this way my

whole life, for I love him and know that, without me, he's like a lost child." As she left me, I could only say, "You are a truly great woman." And she knew that, in this life of continuing renunciation, she too is contacted, is given love which no one can take away from her. "To stand up under the disappointment and to persevere in love *nevertheless*, to experience the limits of the loved person and nevertheless to pronounce love's real message 'You are limitless'—herein lies the greatest act of the human heart. It is called Faithfulness. And it must be practiced in accordance with its own nature right up to the final hour. This requirement means oppression for the heart, darkness and bewilderment to the feelings, particularly when the lack of reciprocation causes us pain, the loved one being unable to bring himself up to what he could and ought to be. Anyone who has truly loved has suffered through this painful experience . . . Real love develops only in faith, in the togetherness which holds fast right up to death."[101]

Thus, all the adjectives and attributes of love are applicable to the love which stems from God. God is rejected love. He is the love which is scorned, desecrated, misused and hated. But He also moves forward toward contact as fulfilled love, as the Resurrected. He is the joy, breadth, splendor and beauty of love. He is felt as the ultimate depth of love which receives an answer. If a man were to renounce reciprocated love completely, he would slowly lose the depth of his Being. He would no longer receive his Self from the other, and it would dwindle and dry up. Since his own Person is acquired through contact, it now suffocates, for such a man is no longer able to mean "everything" here on earth to a You, nor is he affirmed down within the very deepest foundations of his Being, nor is he seen as a unique and irreplaceable individual. He would renounce the unique non-recurring aspect of his Person and, with it, his own Person-Being. Then God Himself can no longer be felt as love, for God comes forward in the affirmation of a man's Person. He affirms the Person ever and anew, loving and pardoning the Person—in a word, bestowing love's grace upon the Person.

The life of love is a giving over of oneself, a receiving of love and a new giving. This life perishes if one's love is not returned. True, a faithful persistence in the situation, even without a return of one's love, is a love which one does, indeed, live. But a full answer found in another person does not conflict with love, and one affirms it, answering it with one's Being. When each of the two loving people finds the basis of his meaningful existence in the You, when a mutual affirmation gives each of them a new Being, then eschatological truth becomes present time—then God, who is love, is present. L. Boros says, "We call God now only the last unconditional concern of man in which not merely a partial domain of human existence is called for, but the totality of the Being of his person."[102]

The Song of Songs in the Old Testament is an allusion to this structure of love wherein God manifests Himself as love. Two attempts to interpret it have gone astray. If the Song of Songs is taken literally, it is a purely secular marriage song. The very fact that it is included in the canon of Scripture precludes our seeing it in such a light. The second interpretation would regard the Song of Songs as allegory, the bride as the Soul and the bridegroom as God, but this is no foundation either originally or in the text itself. Rabbi Akiba, who regarded the Scriptures as sacred, but the Song of Songs as most sacred, felt that *in the depths of love itself* one finds God and experiences Him. "Mysticism" lies in the "loving" contact itself, in the very center of the life of love, and not "this side of" it or "beyond" it. "But do the Scriptures know another expression for *spiritual* life, other than that penetration into Reality, that spontaneous urge of the 'material world'? Can anything be entirely 'whole' which will not admit to being rendered in flesh? Is it strange that . . . the Song of Songs . . . was introduced as the reading at the feast of the Passover?"[103] The Passover is evidence of love, the Lord's passing by, Yahweh's presence as salvation. The Song of Songs makes it abundantly clear that love seeks no reward beyond the return of its love. This relationship is absolute and sufficient unto itself, for indeed God is love. Hans Ur von Balthasar points out that the deepest love requires no other "object." In the Song of Songs the bride and groom have no children. They mean everything to one another, are sufficient to one another, and all fertility lies contained within the circle of their togetherness: *hortus conclusus, fons signatus.*[104]

The Absolute is love, and in Jesus Christ we clearly see that God is love. In love, which is at the same time the brightest light and the darkest night, all objects lose their outlines; without being oppressed by a law or asking for reasons or causes, love is taken as a gift, and knows that no other demand can stand up against it. Love, and love alone, merits our belief. "It is the only authentic thing we have, and nothing else may or must engage our belief. That is what we must bring about, faith's 'work'—recognition of the Prius which is absolute and unobtainable through whatever means one might use. Believe that there is love, absolute love. Opposing all the possible experiences existence may offer . . . opposing

every 'reasonable' notion of God . . . the mystery of Being reveals itself as absolute love,"[105] for God is love.

8 Fulfillment: The Answer to All Questions

Now that we have reached the end of this study, we might
do well to reconsider the road we have traveled. Lucretius and
Sartre, and modern man with Sartre, are concerned about the
question of the meaning of human existence. Their despair
leads them to ask how one may come to terms with life. Both
authors maintain that this question cannot be answered, for
they are fully convinced that any answer at hand is false, a
lie. Freeing oneself from "religion" and the concept of God
bound up with it is the first step toward exposing the thirst-
quenching answers of the myths for what they are—mirages,
like the Fata Morgana. We, too, shun these would-be answers,
for they put a false god into our lives, an idol whose existence is derived from our needs and who is supposed to illuminate and answer our Being. Our existence cannot be
illuminated by a system, a "religion" as such, or by our cling-
ing to the Absurd. The question of why we are alive still demands answering. Usually we satisfy ourselves with would-be
answers and bumble along from disappointment to disappointment, dragging our empty Person through the temporality of our Existence.

Our answer lay basically in our insisting on the unanswered
questions and in our persisting in them, and we had to admit
that an answer involving principles was not readily at hand.
The meaning of existence does not unfold before a host of
questions opening into further questions, nor to one in flight

in search of solutions. No, the final answer is to be found in
steady perseverance in the situation, in active assumption of
the whole question-process of existence, opening oneself in
deepest devotion to the You who approaches me. The meaning of Being turns out to be purely individual, existential, personal. The Unconditional—unavailable when one would have
it but ever there, given again and again as a gift—is present
in all that is subject to condition and question. I become sure
about Final Truth, I know about Yahweh, God, through the
demands of the specific situation, the requirements which
come upon me. God does not go forth out of the lacks in
man and return to him empty, but rather withdraws Himself
from the acquisitive aspect of man's nature, manifesting
Himself and His force in the contact and affirmation of one
human being by another. The unknown God does not appear
out there on the boundary, but in the very heart of life, contacting us here in our neighbor. Does that mean we can count
on His being available in our life, love, joy and happiness? As
long as love and contact represent attempts to assert the Self,
the Other is used and abused as an answer to the question of
one's own existence, and the Absolute abstains from entering,
even in the loving union of oneself with the Other. He who
looks to You for his own happiness is seeking an Object. All
of the striving of love arising from this need to become absolute Subject is a desecration of the Other, and it spells love's
death. No one has brought this home in a more telling manner than Sartre. Disappointment awaits one in the end; the
two lovers, who seek support in each other in the face of
drowning, go under, locked in embrace. But if one of them
is conscious of this egoism and chooses another course, giving
the Other freedom, he walls his Person off, and each party

finds himself referred back into his own unanswered solitude. The Absolute, love in its innermost Being, the Final Depth, is never available to us at our choosing; it is given, a gift manifested in our contact with our neighbor. Human existence is sustained in a paradoxical identity by the unconditional within the conditional, the unavailable within the material, the final within the ephemeral, the answer *within* the question. The openness to question is never done away with. It continues on. But if the demands of a You are answered in a contact- situation, love permeates this openness, God as love is present within it, the ultimate splendor, the final answer. But this means that "the absurd" has attained a meaning, that man, in assuming his absurdity, has found meaning—in contact—and that a loving face appears to the seeker in the depths of the being-with-Another which constitutes his Existence. The loved You becomes one's neighbor, and Jesus Christ is there in one's love for one's neighbor. This is how the final answer comes about: God in the center of our lives. God's word gives the answer—to all questions! Certainly never as a system, never as a method, never as an answer at our beck and call. No, God is there on the road to compassionate love. The more uncompromising the philosophy, the deeper the sense of meaninglessness in man's quest for a final support. And the further does a god of religious feeling fade into an opaque veil. This leaves the existential understanding of man all the freer for the answer *in* the question, the Absolute *in* the contingent, Jesus Christ in one's neighbor, God in man. And the word was flesh— that which one cannot lay his hands on is alive in that which one can have at will. The world devoid of love receives deepest love and devotion. God becomes real in the heart of our lives. Faith and hope come to fruition in love. The answer is self-engendering in the loving contact with Another, and the unknown God, having traveled the entire distance through death and resurrection, returns to man. Isn't Nietzsche's longing directed to Him when he says,

> *My stream of tears all flow to you!*
> *My heart's last flame rekindles!*
> *Return return*
> *Thou unknown God*
> *My pain, my final bliss!*

The "unknown god" has stepped forward from His concealment. He is the God who is love. And in love He reveals Himself to us.

Notes

1 Lucretius, *De Rerum Natura*, Zurich, 1936: I, 55–61; II, 87–93, 241; VI, 34–42. *Nature of the Universe*, by R. E. Latham (Baltimore: Penguin Books, 1965) is one of many fine English translations of *De Rerum Natura*.

2 *Ibid.*, I, 932.
3 *Ibid.*, I, 936–950; IV, 11–25.
4 *Ibid.*, I, 81–82.
5 *Ibid.*, I, 83.
6 *Ibid.*, I, 84–101.
7 *Ibid.*, I, 62–79.
8 *Ibid.*, I, 150; cf. also I, 206, 266.
9 *Ibid.*, V, 1184, 1193.
10 *Ibid.*, VI, 417–432.
11 *Ibid.*, VI, 400ff.
12 *Ibid.*, I, 325–345.
13 *Ibid.*, V, 75ff.
14 *Ibid.*, V, 95–98.

[15] Ibid., I, 215–220; 540–550.

[16] Lucretius, De Rerum Natura, III, 510–614.

[17] Ibid., III, 970–971.

[18] Ibid., III, 894–901.

[19] Ibid., III, 830–831; 926–927.

[20] Ibid., III, 1035–1045.

[21] Ibid., III, 1068–1069.

[22] Ibid., IV, 1058–1072.

[23] Ibid., IV, 1085ff.

[24] Ibid., IV, 1236–1239.

[25] Ibid., IV, 1222.

[26] Ibid., I, 1–61.

[27] Jean-Paul Sartre, L'existentialisme est-il un humanisme?, Paris, 1964, 35–36. Existentialism, the English translation of this work, was published by Philosophical Library, New York, 1947.

[28] Simone de Beauvoir, Die Mandarins von Paris, München, 1960, 37. An English translation, The Mandarins has been published by World Publishing Co., Cleveland, Ohio.

[29] Sartre, Les mouches, Paris, 1943, III, 2. The English translation of passages from this play are from No Exit and The Flies, by permission of Alfred A. Knopf, Inc., copyright, 1946, by Stuart Gilbert.

[30] Ibid.

[31] Ibid.

[32] Sartre, L'existentialisme est-il un humanisme?, 95.

[33] Sartre, L'Etre et le Néant, Paris, 1943, 34.

[34] Sartre, Les mouches, III, 2.

[35] Sartre, La nausée, Paris, 1938, 163. Nausea, by Jean-Paul Sartre and translated by Lloyd Alexander, is published by New Directions Publishing Corporation, New York. Translated passages by permission of New Directions Publishing Corporation.

[36] Ibid., 163–164.

[37] Ibid., 164.

[38] Ibid., 170.

[39] Ibid., 166.

[40] L'Etre et le Néant, cf. 126, 558–559. The English translation, Being and Nothingness, has been published by Citadel Press, New York, 1965.

[41] Ibid., cf. 46–47.

[42] Ibid., 57.

[43] Ibid., 134.

[44] Ibid., 103.

[45] Ibid., cf. 529.

[46] Ibid., cf. 75.

[47] Ibid., 76.

48 *Les mouches*, III, 2.
49 Sartre, *Le diable et le bon Dieu*, Paris, 1951, I, 3, 6. *Devil and the Good Lord*, an English translation, has been published, 1965, by Alfred A. Knopf, New York.
50 *Ibid.*
51 *L'Etre et le Néant*, cf. 515, 565, 639.
52 *Ibid.*, 566.
53 *Les mouches*, cf. III, 2.
54 *L'Etre et le Néant*, 559.
55 *Ibid.*, 193.
56 *Ibid.*, 188.
57 *Ibid.*, cf. 158–159.
58 Sartre, *Les jeux sont faits*, Paris, 1947, 25. *The Chips Are Down*, the English translation, was issued, 1948, by Lear Publishing Company, New York.
59 *L'Etre et le Néant*, 633.
60 *Ibid.*, cf. 624.
61 *Ibid.*, 631.
62 *La nausée*, 163.
63 *L'Etre et le Néant*, 285.
64 *Ibid.*, cf. 303.
65 *Ibid.*, cf. 310–364.
66 *Ibid.*, 341.
67 *Ibid.*, 350.
68 *Le diable et le bon Dieu*, II, 10, 4.
69 *Ibid.*, II, 10, 2.
70 *L'Etre et le Néant*, cf. 430.
71 *Ibid.*, cf. 439.
72 *Ibid.*, 445.
73 *Les jeux sont faits*, 34.
74 *Le diable et le bon Dieu*, I, 3, 6.
75 *Ibid.*, II, 4, 5.
76 *Ibid.*, III, 8, 3.
77 *Ibid.*, cf. II, 5, 4.
78 *Ibid.*, II, 6, 4.
79 *Ibid.*
80 *Ibid.*
81 *Ibid.*, III, 9, 3.
82 *Ibid.*, III, 11, 2.
83 *Ibid.*, III, 10, 2.
84 *Les mouches*, III, 8, 2.
85 *Le diable et le bon Dieu*, I, 1, 1.
86 *Ibid.*
87 *Ibid.*, I, 3, 4.

[88] *Ibid.*, II, 6, 6.

[89] *Ibid.*, III, 8, 2.

[90] *Ibid.*, III, 8, 3.

[91] *Ibid.*, III., 10, 5.

[92] *Ibid.*

[93] *L'Etre et le Néant*, 708.

[94] D. Bonhoeffer, *Widerstand und Ergebung*, Munich, 1962, 242.

[95] K. H Miskotte, *Wenn die Götter schweigen*, Munich, 1963, 128.

[96] M. Noth, *Das 2. Buch Moses*, Göttingen, 1961.

[97] H. Gollwitzer, *Die Existenz Gottes im Bekenntnis des Glaubens*, Munich, 1963. An English translation, *Existence of God as Confessed by Faith*, was published, 1965, by Westminster Press, Philadelphia, Pa.

[98] D. Bonhoeffer, *Widerstand und Ergebung*, Munich, 1962, 242; John A. T. Robinson, *Gott ist anders*, Munich, 1964, 81ff. Bishop Robinson's work originally appeared in English under the title *Honest to God* (Philadelphia: Westminster, 1963). The resultant controversy over *Honest to God* led its publisher to bring out *"Honest to God" Debate*, edited by David L. Edwards.

[99] Cf. Gotthold Hasenhüttl, *Der Glaubensvollzug*, Müchen, 1962, 260–277.

[100] L. Boros, *Der anwesende Gott*, Olten, 1964, 19–20.

[101] *Ibid.*, 23, 77.

[102] *Ibid.*, 53–54.

[104] Cf. Hans Urs von Balthasar, *Prayer*, Sheed & Ward, New York, 1961,
[103] Miskotte, *op. cit.*, 269.
76 ff.

[105] *Ibid.*, 67–68.